Flying OVER Home

Also by Jeanette Stokes

25 Years in the Garden

Hurricane Season: Living Through a Broken Heart

35 Years on the Path

Flying OVER Home

Jeanette Stokes

Words & Spirit
Durham, North Carolina

Flying Over Home
Copyright 2013 © Jeanette Stokes.

Designed by Designing Solutions, LLC
Printed in the United States of America.

ISBN 978-0-9821848-5-1

Library of Congress Control Number: 2013946105

First Edition, 2013
10 9 8 7 6 5 4 3 2 1

Copies of this book may be ordered from:
Words & Spirit
1202 Watts Street
Durham, NC 27701
wordsandspirit@aol.com

For Gail, Beth, and Sharon

Contents

One
The Day My Father Died
1976

A few stray daffodils had already opened by the first of March 1976, and there was a light green wash on some of the trees. Spring was breaking out in Durham, North Carolina, and had been for weeks. The first of March fell on a Tuesday that year, and I, a second-year graduate student at Duke Divinity School, was in the school's Women's Center, where I worked as the director. My redheaded friend and fellow student Marge had just arrived to strategize before our afternoon appointment with the dean. We planned to explain to our serious, justice-minded leader why it was important to have more women on the divinity faculty. We had only one woman teaching at the time, though women made up a quarter of the student body.

Marge and I were standing in the small basement office, which our female professor had relinquished for our use. Since it was near the mailroom and the noisy hub of student life, she was probably just as happy to move to a quieter third-floor retreat. Our office had one tall thin window that looked out on a back entrance to the school, blank sides of a few buildings, and some tall trees in the distance.

When the phone on the desk by the window rang, I picked up the heavy black receiver.

The voice on the other end said, "Jeanette, this is your mother." I was surprised. Though I spoke with her regularly, she never called me at school. "Well, hello," I replied, still too young to dread unexpected phone calls. She may have said something else first, but all I heard was, "Your father died a day or so ago." Something exploded inside of me, as though an airplane door had opened at 30,000 feet and all the air and everything that wasn't strapped down was being sucked out. I was weeping and trying to catch my breath. "Oh," said the calm voice on the other end of the phone. "I forgot this would upset you." With that, my best support flew out the window of the plane along with the pocketbooks, peanuts, and life preservers.

Upset? Had my mother taken leave of her senses? I only had one father. Even if he had been a poor substitute for one in recent years, he was still the only one I had. Upset? I was the kid who couldn't bear to part with her baby dolls! I had already lost him once, well twice, well three times, if you count divorce, alcoholism, and his new family. And I had never gotten used to it.

We finished the conversation with something vague about my needing to decide whether I was coming to Tulsa for the funeral. Funeral? My brain was as mushy as impatiens after a frost; I couldn't think about a funeral. I hung up the cold heavy receiver and turned to Marge. I could hardly get the words out between my gasps for breath, "My father died." I buried my face in Marge's red curls, as she wrapped me up in her arms.

The rest of the afternoon is vague except that Marge was never far from my side. We went ahead with our meeting with the dean where Marge explained the news I had just received. We managed to make our case, and the dean seemed to understand that the women students needed more female role models in the school.

Somehow I got back to my apartment, with Marge's help I suspect. I do remember her saying something about not leaving me alone, an excellent move, which I always attributed to her hospital chaplaincy training. She was certainly being of more use than my family.

Later that afternoon, I called my boyfriend, who was visiting his parents in Greensboro, an hour away. "My father has died," I reported, already exhausted from trying to balance in a world now missing half its foundation. In his kind, slow, southern voice, my boyfriend said, "I'll be there tomorrow." *Tomorrow*? My father had died, for God's sake. *Tomorrow* was six months away. I needed my sweetie right then. But I didn't say, and he didn't know. "OK," I said, as the umpire inside yelled, "Strike three." That made one dead father, one clueless mother, and one useless boyfriend.

Meanwhile, I had to decide whether to go to the funeral. Daddy had been dead a day or so before Mother got the news and called me. I had less than twenty-four hours to decide whether to fly to Tulsa if I wanted to arrive in time for the funeral. For several complicated reasons, I decided not to go.

The words echo in my head, *I did not attend my father's funeral.* I'm the person who shows up for the funeral of nearly everyone else's mother, father, brother, sister, or best friend. I encourage people to go to the funeral of anyone who has meant anything to them. But I didn't attend my father's funeral.

I have no idea how I made the decision. It was during my "I hate flying" period. I suspect that the real reason I didn't go was that there was no one in Tulsa who could help me. My mother wasn't going to help me deal with my father's death, my own grief, or whatever I might experience at the funeral. She had been divorced from him for over a decade and didn't like to think or talk about him. Uncle Henry and Aunt Mary Beth, my father's brother and his wife, attended the funeral, but I didn't know they were going and was not close to them at the time. I had never seen or spoken to my father's third wife. I simply couldn't bridge the gap. If I had it to do over again, I'd beg my friends to drive me to the airport and put me on the plane. I was, however, spared a funeral that my aunt and uncle described for the rest of their lives as the worst thing they had ever attended. Given my father's drinking, gambling, and carousing, I can only imagine the tacky crowd that might have assembled. Daddy had rekindled his childhood religion and could be maudlin when we talked by phone, so who knows what went on. My grief was influenced only by my own experience of disappointment and abandonment and not by the shenanigans of my father's compatriots. Safe in the freezer compartment of my heart, my grief and resentment could stay rock hard until cracked open by a comparable loss in the future. For the time being, my damn father, who had already left me, had up and died. I was as mad and as brokenhearted as a person could be all at once.

That's it in a nutshell. My father left, and then he died, and I didn't go to the funeral. Nothing finished, nothing resolved, and no one to help with any of it until I was grown and bought myself twenty or thirty years of therapy. Even then, it was not until I was blown apart by my own divorce that I could risk admitting that I had loved my father like breath itself, that losing him had nearly destroyed me, and that I had never figured out what to do about the tacit assumption, by so many, that he was a bad person. What in the world could it mean to love and miss someone who was bad? It is probably just as well that, at twelve and thirteen, when he was so newly gone from our family, I went right on focusing on how well my lime green sweater looked with my blue and green plaid skirt and did not pay too close attention to what was happening to the life around me.

* * *

For decades I was not even sure what killed him. If asked, I'd say, "A heart attack or a stroke; he was overweight, drank, and had high blood pressure. You pick the cause." He was a self-proclaimed "bad boy." It could have been anything.

The summer after my father died, I spent six weeks in a feminist theological program at Grailville, a Catholic educational center near Cincinnati, Ohio. One of my projects was to keep a journal of imagined conversations with my father. I can still remember how angry I was that he had been such a mess and then had died. I was nowhere near through with him. There were all kinds of things I needed to know and to sort out with him. Thirty years later it still stuns me that he had the audacity to die. It felt like getting disconnected in the middle of an important conversation. On June 30, 1976, a few months after his death, I wrote,

> Daddy. I don't really like calling him *Daddy*, *Dad*, or even *Father*. Malcolm fits my image of him much better. I can speak of him as "my father" OK. *Daddy* is such a snuggly word, and I don't really want to snuggle him. When I'd hug him, he'd want me to say I loved him, and I didn't, or not in a very snuggly way. I didn't like him, although I cared very much what happened to him. One thing at a

time. Malcolm. E. Malcolm Stokes, MD would have been 59 years old on June 13, 1976. That means he was born in 1917.

He is not the person I would have liked for him to be. We did not understand each other. He was an impractical, irresponsible romantic who wanted to love and to be loved, but I'm not sure he knew how to do either. I wanted to be loved by a wonderful Daddy and to love a wonderful Daddy, but I didn't think him very wonderful. It was disappointing and frustrating. He died in silence, little communication between us. A phone call to say he was married [a third time] and happy about his "cute little wife."

We care about each other, but don't know how to express or share that in any kind of meaningful way. And so he died rather unsatisfied, and I'm rather unsatisfied. We are unforgiven, unsatisfied, unresolved. And I'm mad that he died before we could work it out. I was just beginning to think there might be some hope for us—that being married would make him easier to get along with. But he died and left everyone fighting over him. I think that is the way he intended it. He would like for me to get into the fight, to struggle for a piece of him. But I don't care enough, and I don't feel I deserve enough to fight very hard.

My father lived alone for a year or so after his second wife Faye left and before he married the third time. I had just begun graduate school by then. He'd call me late at night—sad, lonely, and drunk, his words sloshed around and slurred together. I remember he said that being in love was the best thing in the world. He also said that what every man wanted was a twenty-three-year-old woman, which creeped me out, since that was exactly how old I was. I felt like I was the grown-up and he was a college sophomore.

At Grailville in 1976, I also wrote,

There was something unspoken that went on in those last years, when he was so unhappy and so alone [before he was married the third time]. Sometimes I felt like I was the only family he had. There was a funny kind of feeling between us. Even though he was a mess and I wished he'd leave me alone, I loved him. I loved the things I was afraid to remember about him. I love the things that were his and are mine: our bad eyes, small size, perky personality, many talents, determination. Little round fat man with glasses and a crew cut. I wonder if everyone who knew him loved him and hated him as much as I do.

It took twenty years and my own unpleasant divorce for me to stop being so furious at my father and to find new ways to appreciate him. When the screaming pain of losing him finally quieted down, I remembered how much I loved him and how much he loved me. He made a mess of everything, but that didn't take away my sense that my dad had once adored me. I wanted to know more about *that* man, about *that* father.

Divorce sucks. It was clear to me from the beginning of my parents' separation that I was losing my father. I followed my mother's lead and assigned him the role as the bad guy in the story, and tried to act like it was good riddance. But I was as brokenhearted as a person can be and still get up every day and go through the ninth grade. I was mostly interested in my friends, in wearing cool clothes, and in belonging to a social club, so most of the time I did not think about what I had lost. I had my mother's undivided attention and plenty of sympathy from school friends and adults. I tried to ignore the disaster and go right on, which was a big mistake, but I had no way of knowing that at the time.

Family life as I had known it ended with the divorce. Mother and I continued to live in our house for a year. Then she sold the house, gave away our two poodles, and moved us into an apartment. A year later, she got married again, and we moved into my stepfather's house. They gave me a large bedroom and my new six-year-old stepsister a smaller one, but it was still the home of strangers. My family had ended in an explosion that made almost no sound and left me with wounds I would hide from everyone, including myself, for years to come.

Divorce is so bad that I would say it ruined my life, except that my life was not completely ruined. I have had, and continue to have, a fine life. Still, divorce shreds a child's sense of safety. At least it did mine. When I contracted a life-threatening disease at the age of eight, my still-married mother and father were right there in front of me the whole time, doing everything they could to assure me that I was going to be fine. Thanks to good medical care and plenty of entertainment, I survived without being scared out of my wits. But when my parents divorced, they were both so injured by the experience and so caught up in their own lives that whatever reassurance they offered was not very convincing. My mother promised that everything was going to be all right, and from the outside it looked like it was, but the loss I sustained in their break-up turned out to be the central organizing experience of my life.

I had to find out more about the father I had lost and whether I was like him. Maybe then I could salvage the love that had once existed between us and rest from constantly searching for him.

Two
Driving Toward Daddy
2005

When my cousin Sharon e-mailed me in early August 2005 to tell me her brother Jere's cancer had worsened and that hospice had been called in, I knew that I would arrange to attend his funeral. I hadn't been to Macon, Georgia, since I was four and the flower girl in another cousin's wedding. My father had graduated from college there; his brother, my uncle Henry, had served as a Baptist pastor there; and I was dying to know more about the place. I wondered whether Daddy had been involved in music and sports and whether he was as social then as he was later on. My father and all his relatives were from Georgia, but I knew almost nothing about the state. Even though I had lived my adult life only 300 miles from the state line, I had been there only a few times. Even having visited the skyscrapers of Atlanta, I secretly believed the state was still trapped in the nineteenth century.

One of my earliest memories of Georgia is of being in the dark narrow front hall in my grandmother's house in Savannah. I didn't like her very much, my father's mother, and I didn't know her long. She died when I was six, and the few memories I have of her are unpleasant. She was always telling me what to do. "Don't suck your fingers, Jeanette," she'd say, which was useless. I had to be bribed out of sucking my fingers when I was eight years old. I agreed to give up the habit in exchange for a French poodle (that would later be lost in the divorce). "Move back from the television, Jeanette, you'll ruin your eyes," Grandmother would instruct. I'd move back an inch and try to ignore her. I was nearsighted and couldn't see the damn television unless I got right up close to it. If you had felt the tension at our house when my father's parents came to visit, you might have slept on top of the TV and stuffed your whole hand in your mouth.

My mother could hardly tolerate her mother-in-law. The older Mrs. Stokes was insufferable! Mother says that when she and Daddy were first married, there would be a knock at the door and she would find Mr. and Mrs. Stokes on the doorstep, intending to stay for two weeks. My mother had never heard of such a thing.

Grandmother Viola Stokes was the eleventh of eleven children, born to a Confederate farmer in South Georgia who later turned shopkeeper and later still became a traveling whirligig operator. Her mother ran a boardinghouse in Savannah to keep the family fed during the whirligig phase. When I knew her, Viola was a rigid, bossy, aggravating old woman who annoyed people no end. My mother once got so mad at her that she heaved a cast iron skillet at the woman. Never too good at sports, Mother missed. God knows what the older woman had said.

"Malcolm, your mother is crazy," my mother would say. "Netta, she is not crazy," he would insist. When Daddy finally took his mother to see a psychiatrist, the expert agreed with my mother but said Viola was too old to do anything about it.

I was the buffer, or so my father reported to his brother in a letter in October 1954. My grandparents had come to Tulsa for a series of medical checkups, my father the doctor having taken charge of their various health issues. Daddy wrote, "Netta and I have gotten along very well this visit. It has been a little trying at times, of course, as it always is, but under the circumstances I think we have survived admirably. Of course, Jeanette adds a lot by being the sweet child that she is. She keeps peace in the family when things look a little stormy."

* * *

My father had only one sibling, his brother Henry, seven and a half years older. My grandmother insisted from the beginning that Henry would be a preacher and Daddy would be a doctor, and so they were. Henry, tall and stately, graduated from Mercer College and then from Yale Divinity School. (That a Southern Baptist from Savannah would go all the way to New Haven, Connecticut, to seminary suggests how liberal Mercer was at the time.) Henry served churches in Georgia and Tennessee until he left the Baptists over integration. He was for it, while many in his Macon, Georgia congregation were not. After that, he switched to the Episcopal Church and became a priest.

Daddy, who was short, quick, and into everything, went to Duke and then Mercer, studied medicine at the University of Georgia School of Medicine (later known as the Medical College of Georgia), took an internship in New Orleans and then a residency in Dallas. There, he met my mother; they married and moved to Tulsa, which was booming in the 1940s and the perfect place for him to start his practice in obstetrics and gynecology.

After Grandmother died when I was six, my parents never took me to Georgia again. When they split up, I sided with Mother and my Texas relatives and followed their lead in thinking that everything in Georgia was old-fashioned, Baptist, and undesirable, and I nearly lost track of my father's relatives.

* * *

When I learned my cousin Jere had actually died, I packed my bags, got in my relatively new car with a great cup holder and CD player, and headed for Macon. I left Durham at 1:00 pm, hoping to arrive somewhere near Macon by midnight. Since I hated driving on major highways (I-85 through Charlotte and Atlanta, or I-95 to Columbia and then another interstate to the west being the "efficient" ways to approach Macon), I drove south on state highways though Chapel Hill and Pittsboro.

South of Pittsboro, the dark soil turned sandy and hardwoods gave way to whispering pines as I drove on into the Sandhills area, famous for its peaches. Near Southern Pines, the landscape was littered with golf courses, and driving past them, I remembered a picture of my father and his brother posing for the camera, each leaning on a golf club. Daddy was a successful amateur golfer, playing in tournaments at home and abroad. In South Carolina,

I was charmed by a small, well-preserved train station I passed in the tiny town of Patrick. The tidy white building and raised platform looked like something right out of *Fried Green Tomatoes*. I wondered whether my father had ridden the train past towns and stations just like that on his way from Savannah to his first semester at Duke University in 1934. If there had still been decent train service in America in the twenty-first century, I wouldn't have been driving all day by myself to attend a funeral in a nearby state.

I wish I had stopped to take a picture of the hand-painted sign for "Penuts" near Bethune, South Carolina. I love unpretentious, homemade signs. When I crossed into Georgia, I recalled that I once told two elderly Georgia natives that my people were dirt farmers in the southern part of the state. They laughed at how little I knew about their state. One of them said, "Oh honey, after the war, everyone in Georgia was a dirt farmer." She meant the Civil War. As I sped along, I wondered whether my father's people had ever grown peanuts.

I passed Augusta, where my father was a medical student and where the Masters Golf Tournament is played every spring. If I had not been trying to make Macon by midnight, I might have stopped.

I had pictured rural Georgia as flat and boring, so the beauty I encountered was a delightful surprise. Gently rolling farmland and forests stretched out on either side of the road. I listened to Lucinda Williams, Bonnie Raitt, Lyle Lovett, Kate Campbell, and Carrie Newcomer on the CD player and sang along. As the afternoon wore out, the sun became a big red ball that played peek-a-boo with me as it sank behind the trees.

It was dark by the time I passed through Milledgeville, Flannery O'Connor's hometown, and I wondered briefly whether my visit to Georgia would have any of the flavor of her dark stories of morally flawed characters. Milledgeville was about half an hour from Macon and the last place of any size I passed before my destination.

* * *

I arrived in Macon at 9:00 p.m. and made my way to the 1842 Inn on College Street. I had found the inn online before leaving home and called from the road to make a reservation. The receptionist said there was a room for me and that someone would be up until at least 10:00 p.m.

I felt slightly guilty, because my cousins had offered me a sofa to sleep on. I feared an old pattern playing itself out. The doctor's daughter was staying in a nice place while the preacher's kids slept on foldout sofas at their dead brother's house.

Some time later, one of my cousins said that when she was young, her father had explained that *wealth* meant people acted differently. People with wealth (meaning my family) got to stay in a hotel and come over to the house to visit instead of "piling in." I wanted to protest that we were not wealthy, that my father had done it all on credit and always owed more money than he made, but I held my tongue. From my cousin's childhood perspective, we were rich. We stayed in hotels.

That may explain the slight discomfort I felt as I parked in the drive of the Greek Revival antebellum mansion. I got out of the car and climbed the stairs to an enormous *Gone With the Wind* wrap-around porch with a dozen stately white columns, each standing two stories high. Discomfort faded and delight took over at the prospect of spending a night in what looked like a movie set. I was assigned a cozy pink bedroom on the second floor that had its own fireplace. The antique English furnishings, comfortably worn oriental carpet, and queen-size bed welcomed a weary traveler. After writing in my journal and reading for a few minutes, I turned out the ginger-jar lamp beside the bed and went to sleep in my father's native Georgia. Was it more than cotton and slavery, more than faded chintz, bigoted Baptists, and my grandmother's dark front hall? And my father—I was sure he was more than a reckless man who broke my heart, but who was he?

Three
Macon
2005

Well rested, I bounced out of bed the next morning and went for a short walk around the residential area near the inn. The stately antebellum houses in the neighborhood were saved from destruction by Sherman's March only because the general decided to focus his troops on the nearby capital at Milledgeville, which peacefully surrendered. From there the March went on to Savannah and left historic Macon standing for me to enjoy. Perhaps I'd follow Sherman's path from Macon to Savannah next and see the place my father grew up.

Back at the inn, I enjoyed my breakfast in the parlor, with sunlight coming in through tall windows and classical guitar music in the background. As I gazed at an enormous arrangement of flowers on a large round table in the formal entry hall, I tried to picture my aunt and uncle's parsonage in Macon. I could barely remember the large two-story white house with columns from my visit there in December 1955. That's when my oldest cousin Gail got married and I was the flower girl in her wedding. I was four years old, and it was just about the most exciting event of my young life.

I remember posing on the red carpet in the living room in front of the fireplace in Uncle Henry's parsonage. A brass hearth fender dressed up the fireplace behind me. I don't remember the bride, the wedding, or much about the house, but I do remember my dress. The satin was cool and slick under my hands as I smoothed out my skirt, possibly at the instruction of an adult standing nearby. My dress was a pale watery aqua just like the older girls'. I felt like a little princess in my fancy dress and couldn't wait to grow up and be a sophisticated teenager like nine-year-old cousin Sharon, with auburn hair falling to my shoulders in perfect waves.

I have no memory of my father at that wedding. I don't see him in the pictures, though I'm sure he was there. He adored his three nieces and his nephew, and they adored the excitement he brought. "Come on, Sugar, let's go...," he'd say, and off they'd go to the beach or the picture show. I was too busy having my moment in the spotlight to worry about what he was doing. He was simply a reliable presence and not yet a cause for concern. He might have even been the one behind the camera.

Mine is a well-documented childhood. Daddy was always snapping pictures or running his movie camera at birthday parties and family events, and Mother says he loved it when any of us had our picture in the newspaper. Our life together, depicted in those photographs, was safely preserved in scrapbooks and albums, now stored in my closet. I resolved to look more closely at that collection when I got home. Perhaps I could find him or us there.

I gave up the quiet comfort of my breakfast table at the inn, packed, dressed in black, and drove to my dead cousin's apartment. After greeting an assortment of relatives, some familiar and some new to me, I climbed in a car with my cousin Beth, her husband, and her daughter. We chatted quietly as we navigated the streets toward the center of Macon and the historic Christ Episcopal Church. When I asked a question about our grandparents, Beth stopped me with, "Let's not talk about that now." I realized we were headed in slightly different directions. Beth had lost her brother; I was finding my family. My mission could wait.

Back at Jere's apartment after a formal but unremarkable funeral, I ate cold cuts and chatted with cousins and assorted relatives. I struggled to make conversation and felt uncharacteristically awkward. I had hoped people would tell stories or offer opinions about the deceased, but no one was very forthcoming except Jere's sturdy, gritty girlfriend Daryl, who told me Jere was always saying, "Uncle Malcolm this and Uncle Malcolm that. Uncle Malcolm always said...." It pleased me to know that Jere had admired his playful, ambitious, adventurous uncle, but I cringed to think my cousin had tried to use my father as a beacon. Daddy had landed himself in a leaky boat with alcohol, high living, and high blood pressure. Anyone who followed his light could end up dashed against the rocks of life.

Eventually they both did. Daddy crashed when he was only 58; Jere at 62. Jere died of cancer, not of bad living, but the story I tell myself is similar to the one I tell about my dad—a sad life that ended too soon. Inadvertently, my cousin followed my father to an early grave.

I wasn't the only one who seemed uneasy at the gathering after the funeral. Jere's only child, Melissa, was present and appeared to be further out of the family loop than I was. Her mother divorced my cousin when Melissa was quite small and took her so far away that Jere hardly knew her. He had only recently reconnected with his now-grown daughter, and one of his sisters had been keeping Melissa up to date on her father's failing health.

Melissa came to the funeral with her boyfriend, who was, as I recall, interested in cars or motorcycles or something. She was different from my other relatives, and while I knew nothing about her mother, it seemed that the divorce had landed Melissa and her mom in a rough place.

As I pondered this, I realized that my Stokes cousins and I had all been widowed or divorced. All five of us. My parents were divorced and family lore said that our grandparents were also divorced, not from each other, but before they got together. That's a tree with a lot of broken branches, and Melissa may have taken one of the hardest falls.

Before I left Jere's apartment, I got my three female cousins to stand together in Jere's small dining room and snapped a picture of them. Instead of the light colors of Gail's wedding pictures of fifty years before, my cousins were tastefully dressed in black. In the picture, I can see how Gail favors her mother. Beth and Sharon were wearing pearls like the ones I had on that day. Sharon's hair, still as long and lush as in the pictures from decades earlier, had grayed and was pinned up on this occasion.

As I said my goodbyes, I got the address for my father's childhood home in Savannah and headed across Macon to see what I could learn about his college years at Mercer. I wondered whether he had been the life of the party all those years ago.

Four
Mercer
2005

My father graduated from Mercer College in Macon in 1938.
Now known as Mercer University, the school was affiliated with
the Southern Baptists until 2005. He began his college career at
Duke University, in Durham, North Carolina, where I live, but
transferred to Mercer after two years when some infraction on his
part caused his mother to yank him closer to home. That could
have been the time she got mad at him over a car. Daddy worked as
a lifeguard and saved enough money to buy himself a convertible,
but since convertibles were the work of the devil, Grandmother
took the car, sold it, and kept the money. For whatever reason, my
father returned to Georgia and entered Mercer as a junior in the
fall of 1936.

Several years before, I had been to the archives at Duke in search
of pictures of my dad and especially liked the one of him with the
Duke swim team, then known as the *Mermen*. My father stands
upright in his swim trunks, shoulders squarely facing the camera,
head turned all the way to one side, as if meeting a challenge with,
"Bring it on, I can handle it."

After the funeral in Macon in 2005, I drove down College Street
in the direction my cousins had indicated, excited to see another
place where my father spent his young adult years. I knew almost
nothing about Mercer and hoped that seeing the school might offer
some clue about my father as a young man. I wondered whether he
was as gregarious then as I knew him to be later on.

A sign at the corner of College and Coleman Streets announced,
"Mercer University, Founded 1833, Historic Quad North." I

parked my car at the edge of the college, beside a large open green labeled *Tattnall Square Park*. I had heard of Tattnall Square Baptist Church and the deacons who blocked the entrance to an African American man one Sunday morning in 1966.

I found my way to the Jack Tarver Library, a modern brick building on the far side of the campus. Once inside, I headed straight for the archives. It was ten minutes to five, and the Special Collections Assistant was closing up for the day. When I explained that my father graduated from Mercer in 1938 and that I lived in another state, she quickly gathered yearbooks, annuals, and old newspapers for me to take to a reading area on the main floor. She photocopied a few pages from the yearbook for me to keep and pointed to one picture as she handed me the copies. "I see your father was in Jack Tarver's class." It took me a minute to make the connection—I was standing in the archives of the Jack Tarver Library. When I looked him up later, I learned that Jack Tarver was the publisher of *The Atlanta Journal-Constitution* and the chair of the Associated Press.

Back downstairs, I spread the books and papers out on a large table in a well-lit spot and took a deep breath. The archivist suggested I would find more pictures and some of my father's writing.

I opened my father's 1938 yearbook to the pictures of the ninety-three seniors in the graduating class. Eight formal photos were arranged on the right-hand page with names and activities on the facing page. Bold letters spelling "Mercer" ran down the center of one page and "College" down the other. Seven males and one female, all from Georgia, four of those from Macon.

Daddy appears in the upper right-hand corner of one page, just above Bert Struby. "Stokes, E. Malcom, Pre. Med.," says the type to the left of the picture. The "E" stands for Elmer, which he never used. I chuckled when I noticed his name was misspelled. I still have trouble spelling *Malcolm* and always have to remind myself it's not like *welcome*.

My father's eyes twinkle, and he wears the same half-smile I recognize from younger pictures of him. His hair, short and brown, is combed away from his face but is not as slicked down as the other guys'. Round, rimless glasses frame his light-colored eyes, which I remember as green, and he looks snappy in a wide-lapelled herringbone sport coat, striped shirt, and patterned tie. If the seven men on the page asked me out for a date, I'd take the cute one in the glasses.

The youngest-looking student on the page, Daddy was only twenty when he graduated on June 6, 1938. He turned twenty-one the next week. The description with his picture includes my father's activities.

Stokes, E. Malcom [*sic*], Pre. Med.
Savannah, Ga.
Phi Delta Theta; Ciceronian Literary Society; Mercer Players; Glee Club; Cluster Staff, 3, 4; Bear Skin Staff, 3; Cross-Country Team, 3, 4; Tennis Team, 3, 4, Captain, 4; International Relations Club

He was in a fraternity, which explains how he and Mother could have been pinned in 1943. On the Phi Delt page, I notice John M. Couric, television anchor Katie Couric's father. My father stands on the front row of the all-male Glee Club Chorus. At five feet six inches, he fits right in with the other short guys dressed in tuxedoes, white shirts, and bow ties.

It took thirty-three students to publish *The Cluster*, the weekly student newspaper, only two of whom were women. The sports staff included Jack Tarver, John M. Couric, and my father, who loved sports of all kinds. Daddy is depicted as "Number One Player" on the five-man tennis team. He was on the ten-man cross-country team, which had only one meet, "a triangular contest with Auburn and Davidson held between halves of the Mercer-Oglethorpe football game on Homecoming day," which Mercer lost. The student newspaper reported that my father also played golf for Mercer, but not always successfully.

I'm sure Daddy liked to win, but as I remember, what he most wanted to do was to play the game. Rarely a perfectionist (except in the operating room, I hope) he convinced me that if you didn't get it right the first time, you should just try again.

It cost $444 to attend Mercer and live on campus for the academic year 1937–38, and my father certainly got his money's worth. In addition to sports, he participated in theater productions, in a debate and public-speaking group, and was Associate Editor of the *Bear Skin*, the humor magazine. I know he enjoyed telling stories, usually with a glass in his hand, and I'll never forget a set of cocktail napkins he'd give out at our house with cartoon drawings of Eggbert the wisecracking fetus.

I take all of his college activity as proof that my father would try anything: sports, music, theater, writing, you name it. The man I knew thirty years later was just the same. If there were people doing something and it looked like fun, my father wanted to be in the middle of it.

Five
Savannah
2005

It was almost 6:00 p.m. when I left Macon, heading east toward
Savannah, my father's childhood home. I watched the sunset in my
rearview mirror and arrived in Savannah at 9:00 p.m. in the dark.
I felt certain that if I could find the historic district and the huge
park in the middle of town, I'd be able to find a room in a hotel or
inn nearby. It was August, after all, and a person would have to be
out of her mind (or attending a family funeral) to choose that part
of the year to visit a hot, muggy, southern coastal city.

I took an exit marked "37th Street" and drove straight to my
grandmother's house at 301 W. 37th. Though I couldn't see much
in the dark, the narrow two-story clapboard with a front porch on
the corner lot appeared more spacious than I remembered. The street
had a median, which my mother said had been filled with azaleas.
My headlights revealed mostly bare ground, an occasional scraggly
bush, and a few trees. Some houses and yards were in pretty good
shape, while others appeared to be neglected. I made two passes
by the house and headed for lower street numbers and the tourist
containment area; I could come back to the house in the daylight.

I bumped into Forsyth Park within half a mile, which made me
wonder whether my father had played there. It would have been
a very short bike ride or a fifteen-minute walk for him. I imagined
him in knickers, running across an open lawn chasing a ball
thrown by an older boy in a cap and long pants. I drove around
the long rectangular park a couple of times to get my bearings.
Stately mansions flanked the park on three sides. Some appeared
to be private homes, while others had signs indicating they were
inns or hotels, but most looked shut up for the night. I pulled into

the driveway of a well-lit hotel and explained I was looking for a charming, historic bed & breakfast. The clerk suggested a related inn in the historic district and called to arrange a room. It was going to cost the earth for one night, but I was alone in a strange city at night. Good excuse!

Winding my way around Savannah's landscaped squares, I made my way to the Kehoe House on Columbia Square, parked my car, and got out. That's when it hit me. Good God, it was hot as blue blazes at 10:00 pm. It must have been 90 degrees. A gaggle of tourists crossed the small square in front of the inn. Those people were even crazier than I was; they were out wandering around in the heat.

As I locked my car and remarked to myself on the gluey consistency of the air, I remembered a comment my father had made the chilly spring he came to Smith College for parents' weekend. "No wonder Yankees are so crazy. They can't go outside six months out of the year." If Savannah was this hot in August, I wondered whether it ever even got cold.

A narrow center hall held a small reception desk and a pleasant woman who said she had been expecting me. To my left a heavy oak banister guarded the longest, steepest staircase I had ever seen. I imagined some child putting the family cat in a baby carriage at the top of those stairs and letting it fly. After seeing my room on the second floor, I began the sweaty trips up and down the formidable stairs, carrying my suitcase, pillows, and computer.

My bedroom was enormous, with impossibly high ceilings, a king-size bed, the largest armoire in captivity, and a bay of three gigantic windows. Even with the furniture, there was still enough open floor space left for a small yoga class.

Lying in bed in my oversized room, I was too excited to sleep. Once again, I felt as though I had moved onto the set of a fairy tale. Though I knew my father never stayed in places like that as a child, he certainly made every effort to enjoy such luxury once he was grown. Given a choice between a fairy tale and real life, he'd head straight for the princess with the tiny feet.

Morning came without enough sleep, a minor inconvenience. I had one day in Savannah, and I was determined to make the best of it, so I went out for a walk. I wanted to experience as much of my father's hometown as I could.

Making my way through the streets of old Savannah, I passed antebellum, Victorian, and Edwardian mansions standing in rows like ladies in their ball gowns. Iron fences, green grass, flowers, palm trees, and giant hardwoods adorned the tiny lawns. One house with a courtyard and balconies reminded me of an early scene in *Midnight in the Garden of Good & Evil*, when the narrator, a journalist from out of town, first arrives in Savannah.

I walked through Forsyth Park to West Jones Street to find my grandparents' first home. My cousins had told me that if I stood in front of Mrs. Wilkes' Dining Room and looked across the street, I'd be looking at the house. Famous for her Lowcountry food, Mrs. Wilkes served fried chicken, greens, and cornbread to locals and tourists for over fifty-five years, and, after her death in 2002, the restaurant kept up the tradition. I poked my head in the open door and waved to a woman arranging silverware and napkins on tables in the large empty dining hall. Inviting smells that drifted out from the kitchen made me want to sit down, slather butter on a biscuit, and stuff it in my mouth, but they weren't open yet. A long line of tourists hungry for lunch would be forming in just a few hours.

Back outside, the low trees lining West Jones Street offered the illusion of a cool shady lane, though it was already as hot outside as it was in Mrs. Wilkes' kitchen. Two- and three-story brick townhouses stood cheek by jowl on the far side of the street. As I stood in front of Mrs. Wilkes' staring across the street, a young woman drove up in front of a shop on the corner to my right. She got out of her car, unlocked the heavy glass door, and disappeared inside. I held my position, trying to divine which of the nearly identical dwellings might have contained my newly married grandparents.

Another woman, nearer my age, wearing a dark suit and pulling a weighty valise on wheels, approached the shop. She had the worn look that sleeping in motels and eating restaurant food leaves on even the most cheerful of traveling salespeople. We nodded at one another, and I moved in her direction to greet her, mostly so that I'd stop looking like a crazy woman in running shorts staring into space.

I told her I thought my grandparents had lived in one of the houses on that block in about 1915. She asked where I was from, and I said I was just in Macon for a funeral and had driven over to Savannah. "Whose funeral?" she asked. "My cousin Jere Stokes." She said she lived in Macon and had read of his death in the paper. She knew Jere's girlfriend Daryl and had seen her recently using a cane and "not looking so good."

Anyone who knows me would say that greeting a total stranger on the street in an unfamiliar city is exactly what I would do. Friends tease me that I know everyone in town, which is simply not true. If anything unusual happens outside our office, my officemates say, "Send Jeanette, she'll find out what's going on." I have often thought that my father must have passed on to me his curiosity and openness to strangers.

I often wonder why people from Savannah are so friendly. Is it because there are so many black people, and even after decades of cruelty, the good humor of West Africans prevails? Is it because the winter weather is mild enough so people don't have to be in a bad mood for months like up North? But the heat of summer could make Mary Poppins cranky. So what is it? Is it a friendly patina that developed over the top of one of the cruelest systems of control and torture known to humankind? Was it because there was enough money in Charleston and Savannah to make lots of people happy? These people lost the War Between the States and were nearly all reduced to abject poverty, black and white, 140 years ago. Why are they in such a good mood all the time?

I don't know. But I feel it in the friendliness of my cousin Gail; I recognize it in Savannah; and I remember it in my father. It's a warmth that is not trying to hold onto anything too tightly. An extended hand that steps off the porch to greet the stranger. As one man who knew my father used to say, "I wish I could be everybody's friend like Malcolm."

Six
37ᵗʰ Street
2005

After checking out of the Kehoe House, I returned to 37ᵗʰ Street and the "Victorian District." I wasn't sure what I wanted from Savannah, but I was sure I wanted to take a picture of the house where my father grew up. I thought that a photo would be enough for me, something to focus on when I thought about Daddy's childhood. I parked across the street from the house to take a picture, but when I got out of the car, I noticed the front door was just closing. It was not merely a house. It was a house with a person in it!

The last time I had seen the house was in the summer of 1957. I have pictures of myself with relatives at a nearby beach, which means we were visiting in Savannah. I had vague memories of the house itself, mainly of a close dark hallway. Once when my cousin Sharon was in Durham in the 1980s, she mentioned the narrow front hall. That's when I learned she had always wanted our grandmother's doll with the china head that my father scooped up for me when his mother died. As a child, Sharon would stand before the glass-front china cabinet that stood in the hall and long for the doll she was told never to touch. I should have given the doll to her at some point and don't really understand why I have held onto it. Perhaps I've clung to it as replacement for what we both really wanted: a sane grandmother. My father's mother was nuts.

I rushed across 37ᵗʰ Street and its neglected median and up onto the porch of Grandmother's house. Taking a deep breath, I knocked on the heavy metal screen door. An older African American woman in a sleeveless summer top appeared and opened the inside door, leaving the security door locked between us.

"I'm sorry to bother you," I said. "I'm Jeanette Stokes and I think my father grew up in this house."

"Of course he did. Let me get the key," she said as she disappeared into the dark interior.

What good fortune! It hadn't occurred to me that I might get to see the inside of the house. I wondered whether seeing the actual rooms might reveal anything about my father or his family. Would it tell me why my grandmother was so unreasonable or how my father got to be so mischievous?

The older woman returned and opened the door.

"Thank you so much," I chirped as I stepped into the narrow hall I had tried for years to conjure in my mind.

"My father bought this house from your grandfather in 1965," said the woman who had let me in.

Her name was Frances Futch Jenkins. Her father, Gordon Futch, bought the house in March of 1965 and lived there until he died in 1969. Mrs. Jenkins moved in with her family, raised three children in the house, and now has grandchildren and great-grandchildren who visit. It pleased me to think there were more people who had called it "grandmother's house."

Mrs. Jenkins offered to show me around. It was almost midday, and the house was hot and muggy. Though I saw at least one large window unit, there was no air conditioning running. I guess it cost too much and she could stand the heat, but I wondered how. Electric fans hummed in several of the rooms we walked through, moving the sticky air around just as they might have when my father was a boy.

When we passed the staircase in the hall, I imagined Daddy scrambling up the steep stairs as a child. I have no memory of the upstairs bedrooms, and Mrs. Jenkins did not invite me to see them. She had made a tiny bedroom for herself in the back hall, and I sensed that she only used the first floor of the house. Perhaps when family came to visit, they slept upstairs.

I had not remembered that the hall was actually in two parts. The front part served as a vestibule with the living room through a door to the left. A doorway halfway down the hall divided it into two sections. The delicately carved transom overhead allowed air to move about the house even when the green curtain in the doorway was closed. The back part of the hall led to the large dining room and the kitchen at the back of the house. I looked into the dining room and pictured the chandelier that once hung over the dining room table, a glass Tiffany-style shade adorned with green leaves, purple grapes, and other fruits in shades of yellow and orange. At some point my father carried the glass fixture out of the 37th Street house and installed it over the dining room table in the house he built in Tulsa when I was eight. I still regret that my mother sold the lamp with the house after she and my father divorced. I liked the fixture, and I seem to think that if I still had it, I might understand more about the people who once lived in that house.

The living room and dining room fireplaces backed up to each other, sharing a chimney, and were faced with narrow mottled Victorian tiles, white in the living room and a greenish yellow in the dining room. I wondered if it ever got cold enough in Savannah to warrant lighting a fire.

My cousin Gail had reminded me that our grandmother ran a boardinghouse in this house. She remembers an enormous sign in front of the house that announced the "Azalea Tourist Home." My grandmother rented rooms by the night to visitors. She must have learned the trade from her mother, whose home on Jones Street was a boarding house. I wondered where guests would have slept and tried to imagine the dining room as a bedroom for lodgers or for my grandparents.

Mrs. Jenkins and I reached the back of the house and the kitchen, which had not been renovated and probably retained the shape and feel of my grandmother's day. It was a perfectly serviceable kitchen, large enough to accommodate a table. With people sleeping in the dining room, my father must have eaten many of his meals at a kitchen table. I tried to imagine my father and his brother sitting there eating some sort of stew. When I knew him, my father hated stews and casseroles. Mother explained he had eaten too much unidentifiable food during the Depression. Henceforth, he wanted the meat, potatoes, and vegetables to stand separately on his plate.

A kitchen window faced the alley behind the house, and through it I could see a stark backyard with a concrete pad at the rear of the lot. Mrs. Jenkins explained that there used to be shade trees and a garage, but they all wore out and had to come down. Two big trees in front of the house and one on the side were also missing and would have cooled the house and softened the landscape.

Seeing Mrs. Jenkins in her kitchen reminded me of another African American woman who had stood in that same room. Back home, I had a small black and white photograph of a stout African American woman that came with some other family pictures my Georgia cousins had sent. On the back is written in Viola's hand, "71 year old Maggie Seabrook, 549 Park Ave. E, Savannah, GA, July 1944, Malcolm's and Henry's nurse."

July 1944. My mother and father had just gotten married in Texas and were living in Dallas. America was at war. My father was not in the military, because he kept getting deferments for his medical training and then a teaching appointment in Dallas. He wanted to be in the service, but it never worked out until the early 1950s and the Korean War.

In 1944 in Savannah, Maggie Seabrook posed for a picture in front of a wide-board fence that stood as high as she did, with a bush and a tree some distance beyond the fence. Her short hair framed an expressionless face, kind and stern at the same time, reminding me of the loving but firm manner in which black women in the South trained and protected their own from the constant threat of violence at the hands of white men.

Jim Crow ruled the South in 1944 just as it had since the turn of the century when ruling-class white men wrested power from the emerging black electorate by fraud, terrorism, and murder. As historian Tim Tyson likes to say, "The ones with the biggest piles of guns and money usually won."

Maggie Seabrook's wide shoulders are covered by a short-sleeved cotton shirt of a solid color that is simply gray in the photograph.

Her long, dark, carefully pressed skirt hangs to her lower calves. Her ankles and feet are all but obscured by scraggly grass that needs to be mowed.

I wonder whether, at seventy-one, she still worked for my grandmother and grandfather. Was she at their house when a member of the Stokes family snapped the portrait? Did she come over to see my Dad when he visited? How did my grandmother come to have the picture? Had she provided some of the love and warmth that Grandmother had lacked? I could only guess. My cousins knew nothing about this woman.

Maggie Seabrook faces straight into the camera, as if to say, "Come on, future. 'I don't believe He brought me this far to leave me.'" Her hands hang straight by her thighs, the way she was taught to stand quietly, as a girl, at church and school. Her wide hips once carried my father.

Speak to me, Maggie Seabrook. What was it like to be born into freedom in the uncertain days following the end of the Civil War? What was it like to live in Savannah in the early decades of the twentieth century? Did you have to leave your own children to care for two white boys? Did you hold my father with more warmth and kindness than his mother could? What kind of child was my father? Did he make you laugh? Did he aim to please, or did he cover his transgressions with a winning smile?

* * *

I drove straight to Forsyth Park, where Daddy probably played as a child, grabbed my journal and got out of the car, found a bench, and sat down. I was so excited to have been in the house where my father grew up, to imagine him dropping skates or a bike on the porch, letting the screen door bang on the way inside, or reading in his bed upstairs. I admired my surroundings. The central fountain was magnificent with water spraying out in every direction. Birds flew from the fountain to the huge live oak trees and back again. The trees, dripping with Spanish moss, flanked the wide walkway from the fountain to the edge of the park and the street lined with palm trees.

It was hot. I was sitting perfectly still in good shade, and I was covered with sweat. Even the slightest movement of air brought relief. Two elderly black women sat on a bench across the walk from me. From watching them, I learned that if I sat really still, I could be almost comfortable.

My father was born in Savannah in 1917. When he died in 1976, he was only 58. I wondered if the heat had ever bothered him. We had always had air conditioning in Oklahoma, but I seem to remember he was willing to play golf any time of the year.

I was as happy sitting in the park staring at the overhanging trees and the fountain as I had once been gazing at the statue of David in Florence. Out on the street, cars honked and roared their engines, but in the park dappled sunlight fell across the sidewalk and an occasional puff of air cooled my neck. I made a sketch in my journal of a street lamp and its garbage can.

I admired the curve of a distant branch, the shades of green below it, and the deep black skin of the women across the way. One wore a purple shirt and a turquoise flowered skirt, the other a tan shirt and a long brown skirt with small tan flowers. They were getting up to leave. Ms. Purple used a brown metal cane to help her rise and walked slowly away from the fountain.

Sweat dripped from my forehead, but I didn't have a bandana, a clean handkerchief, or even a fan. If I had lived in that climate, I might have known better. Tree frogs started up a chorus with that flat buzzing sound of theirs. Or were they cicadas? I never know.

I stood up to catch the breeze. Now that it was lunchtime, there were lots of people on foot, biking, and walking dogs. A woman jogged past me, ambitious in the heat. It was a well-used park. I had seen people walking around it the night before when I arrived and again in the early morning on my walk.

I had experienced enough of the heat and I had to pee, so I drove to a health food store at the far end of the park. I bought an avocado sandwich on soft bread from the deli in the back of the store and sat on a stool at a bar in the front window to eat. Looking out on the street and the park beyond, I wondered what to do next. I only had that one day in my father's hometown, and I didn't want to miss anything important.

People in Savannah had been nice to me. At the inn, a black woman who was cleaning had seen me peeking in one of the guest rooms. I tried to cover my behavior with, "I'm just poking around," but she said, "Help yourself. Help yourself all you want." Everyone who passed me on my morning walk had said *hey* or *hello*. It was clear to me from this visit that my father was from a friendly city. What else did I want to know?

My belongings were in the car; I could head for the highway and home. I didn't want to drive long into the night, but I wasn't ready to leave the area. I had come this far and really wanted to find out why I had been so attracted to that old Tybee Island photograph, the one of my dad, his relatives, and me. What if going to the beach had made my father who he was? I couldn't leave the area without taking a look.

Seven
Tybee Island
2005

I'm scowling in the faded Polaroid picture from August 1957.
I'm standing in front of my father on the wide flat beach at Tybee
Island. Aunt Mary Beth, Uncle Henry, and three of my four cousins
are lined up beside Daddy. Mother must have been holding the
camera. She appears in other pictures. Everyone has wet hair; we've
been in the ocean. I'm pretty cute in my bathing suit with the busy
ruffle along the bodice, but I'm clearly irritated, as if interrupted
while making important art in the sand.

I used a copy of that picture in a piece of art I made in a Carol
Owen workshop in the summer of 2005. I had first admired Carol's
miniature buildings, which she calls *spirit houses*, on a visit to
her studio south of Chapel Hill a few years before. Since the little
structures were made of simple materials—foam core, rice paper,
diluted paint, maps, old letters, and family photos—I thought
I could make one myself. But when I tried, what I produced
was ugly. So when I heard that Carol was giving a workshop in
Durham, I signed up.

The instructions said to bring family photographs, letters, and
trinkets, so I grabbed a few pictures of my parents and other
relatives on my way out the door.

On the first day of the two-day workshop, I sat at a folding table
and happily measured, cut, and glued together a small foam core
building. A shallow cabinet, ten inches high and six inches wide, it
had a picture frame door and a long drawer at the base.

On the second day, I made Xerox copies of materials I had brought:
a map of Georgia, a picture of my father as a child at Niagara Falls,

one of me on a diving board with my father in the water below, and the one on the beach at Tybee Island. I glued the pictures onto my spirit house, with the beach one as the focal point.

I didn't really plan my spirit house—I just grabbed things and stuck them on, but later it seemed as if I had been leaving clues for myself. Weeks later when I looked at the little house, the message was clear. I had painted the whole thing turquoise. The map included Savannah and the coast of Georgia, and the pictures were of the beach, the ocean, a waterfall, and a swimming pool. The message was clearly, "Jeanette, notice the water!"

My father loved the water, but I had not noticed that until I pasted bits of history onto a box and called it a shrine. Daddy's family didn't have much money, and the Depression hit when he was a teenager. If he could get a ride, the ocean was only eighteen miles away. And there was a YMCA in Savannah where he probably swam.

* * *

The half-hour drive from Savannah to Tybee Island was gorgeous, passing through marshy country with pools of water and patches of grasses and reeds. Tybee looked like a place where people live as well as vacation. Small roads crisscross neighborhoods of one-story houses, palm trees, and oleander. If you don't know oleander, it's a fluffy bush with long thin leaves and small flowers, usually pink or white, like a big azalea bush with weeping willow leaves. My father used to tell a story about how the bush got its name. When a boy named Leander brought his girlfriend a bunch of flowers clipped from this bush, she exclaimed, "Oh, Leander!" I now suspected that oleander was part of my father's childhood and wondered whether he knew the bush was poisonous. Every part of the oleander is toxic. *Beauty, danger, Daddy*—it was a fleeting thought.

I parked my car at the road's sandy edge and walked the long boardwalk to the beach. I took my shoes off, stepped onto the hot, white, hard-packed sand, and walked to the water's edge. The gently sloshing ocean was as warm as bathwater. It was mid-afternoon and scorching hot, and there were few people out. The houses and buildings that lined the beach reminded me of the North Carolina coast. I snapped a few pictures of the sea and then set my camera on the boardwalk railing and took a picture of myself. I wanted to get in the water, but I was alone and in a hurry.

I now think of my father nearly every time I get in the ocean. He was totally competent in the water, completely at home. A small, physically coordinated man, he was a great swimmer and diver. I was in lakes and pools with him many times, and in the ocean a few. When they dammed up a river in eastern Oklahoma to form Grand Lake, he took Mother and me to see it. He and my mother built a house with a swimming pool, and after their divorce he built a house on a lake.

He was determined I would learn to swim at an early age. I remember paddling around with Pixie, a family friend who had a backyard pool. I think Daddy arranged for her to teach me to swim. By the time I was nine, we had moved into a house with our own pool. Since it was frying hot in Tulsa in the summer, I was frequently in the water. To this day, water is a comfort. I often feel that if I can just get in the water, everything will be all right.

I decided to do an experiment one September afternoon a few years ago when I was at the beach for a writing retreat. I got in the ocean to see if I would feel or remember anything about my dad. I wanted someone to go with me, but everyone else was resting or writing. So I went by myself. With few people on the beach, I asked a woman resting on a towel if she'd watch me. I didn't even ask if she could swim, but she looked like someone who could yell for help if I got into trouble.

I waded in, jumping up every now and then to keep the small waves from drenching me. The water was cool on my skin, but in no time I was swimming up and down in the silky sea. When I asked myself how I felt, sadness began to rise in me. I wanted my father. I wanted him right beside me, bobbing around, being silly, teasing me, swimming under water and surprising me, frolicking like a dolphin. I missed my Daddy.

I lost many things in my parents' divorce, some of which were obvious immediately, and some have taken me decades to notice. I lost live music in the house, a menagerie of pets, and my swimming buddy. Now I make sure to buy tickets to live concerts several times a year. I joined a water aerobics class at the YMCA, which ensures that I get in a pool once a week. And I go to the beach several times a year with some sturdy women friends who love the ocean. When we are splashing around together, I enjoy myself and almost forget to miss my dad.

But I don't forget. Every time I get in the water, I remember my father, and I miss him all over again.

* * *

Tired but satisfied with my quick trip to Georgia, I got back in my car, turned up the air conditioning, and headed north. It seemed like a good beginning to my efforts to discover more about my dad. By 8:00 p.m. when I pulled into a rest stop on I-95, I was well into North Carolina and felt somewhat encouraged by an almost-full moon that had risen in the east. I had arrived in Macon in the dark. I would return home, still in the dark, but with a sense of my father coming into focus, as when someone walks toward me on a beach lit only by the moon.

Eight

The City of New Orleans
1943

When my cousins were going through Uncle Henry's papers, they found a folder marked "Malcolm" containing two dozen letters my father wrote to his brother in the early 1940s. Beth sent me the letters in the spring of 2000, just before my forty-ninth birthday. Reading about my father in his own words, poorly typed on a manual typewriter, I laughed and wept. It felt like turning back the clock and meeting him as a young man, full of ambition, energy, and mischief.

He had finished his training at the University of Georgia Medical College in Augusta and followed a buddy to New Orleans for an internship at Charity Hospital. The letters contain references to his attempts to get into the war, meeting my mother, getting married, and moving to Tulsa. In the early ones, Daddy was a twenty-five-year-old intern; the later ones are written from Dallas and Tulsa.

In the first letter, written on a Thursday in January of 1943, Daddy is wishing his brother a happy thirty-third birthday. The letterhead is from "Charity Hospital of Louisiana at New Orleans." He mentions sending money and a box of gifts for Henry's family and apologizes for not sending Christmas presents, blaming that oversight on his recent "bereavement." Some love interest didn't work out, and he notes, "as they say unlucky in love and lucky in other things," which he had been. This was before he met my mother.

He writes that he is on "the accident room service" and enjoying it.

> I worked days for two weeks and am on nights now. At Christmas time I was swamped which was the reason I

didn't get to even send you a thing. But please don't be mad. I guess I am sort of irresponsible anyway. Say, that bathrobe was *swell*. I didn't have a good one and it will come in real handy.

His use of the word *swell* amuses me. It sounds like the 1940s, and it was. I recognize my father's hit-or-miss approach to holidays. He was generous, when he remembered or got around to it. The letter goes on to describe his adventures in New Orleans. The city of jazz and Mardi Gras was the perfect place for a young professional with a wild streak.

Henry, I might fly over to see you next month some time. If my luck holds out and it can't change much because I hve [*sic*] it sewed up. I am a bad boy I reckon. I have won over one thousand dollars in the last ten days. I have 500 dollars worth of war bonds and 300 in the savings account at the bank. Please don't tell anyone and destroy this letter. I hit a long shot at the race track. Started with two dollars and parleyed it on up to what it is now. So keep it a secret please and pray that no ill befalls me.

Remember, they were Baptists. Daddy notes that he has bought a radio for himself and some other things he wanted and that he was thinking of sending something to his mother and father, but not so much that they would suspect his good fortune.

That's the man I knew—up for any adventure, willing to take a risk, and generous. Later that spring, he bought a boat.

Yes, I bought a sailboat with another boy with the last of my little extra money, and I think it is the best investment I have ever made. It is a twenty foot sloop and carries about ten people. We go out on the lake all the time and have a grand time on it, although for awhile I wasn't such a good sailor and ran into the rocks and lighthouse and had to be pulled in by the coast guard [*sic*].

In a letter written on a Sunday in March 1943, he reports on his medical training.

I have been getting along fine but working at night is mighty tedious. I can deliver babies better than I used to. I helped do one Caesarian section the other night.

Time flies on. I only have 3 1/2 months of internship. I might stay on here as a resident in Ob. & Gyn. I sort of like the work. I believe that is the best they have down here, too.

My penmanship gets worse as time goes on. However, my sewing improves. I repaired an episiotomy (if you know what that is) in eight minutes the other night.

He was ever enthusiastic about what he was learning in his internship. In June he says:

I am on an anesthesia service this month, giving anesthetics for the patients to go to sleep. It is very interesting work. I also get to see a lot of operating and that is also good; I think I am going to be on surgery next year.

Fifty years later, my mother's comment about my father's year in New Orleans was, "Boy, he had a good time in New Orleans." She remembered that he played the horses and won a bunch of money. "He'd go to the races and they'd all give him money to bet, all the interns and nurses." She also said he had a good time riding the ambulance. It was a huge charity hospital, and they brought in people from miles around. "He had a good time down there. It was a wild place."

I don't know how wild it was, but from the following story Daddy told about his car, it seemed anything but calm.

My little car has really been taking a beating down here. A truck knocked my hood crooked, someone stole my gas ration book and other stuff out of the compartment and now someone has beaten in my taillight. However, it still runs good and I have 35,000 miles on it.

Nine
Full Court Press
Dallas, 1944

Eventually my father had his fill of the high life and excitement of the city of jazz, and the dank underside of New Orleans began to wear on him. Sandy, another intern, was returning home to Dallas for his residency and encouraged my father to "come on down." He said that with Baylor and the new Southwestern Medical School at Parkland, they would find something for Daddy to do until he could get in the military. So my father went to Dallas and got accepted as an ob/gyn resident at Parkland.

Daddy was trying feverishly to get into the Navy. Henry used a connection he had, but when they nearly had everything lined up, "procurement and assignment" froze my father to his job in Dallas without his ever being enlisted. There were so few doctors that they needed him to keep teaching in the medical school. He stayed in Dallas three years and somehow managed to teach and finish his residency at Parkland at the same time. On August 14, 1943, he writes to Henry.

> The state procurment [*sic*] and assignment won't let me go now as they designate me as essential to this new school. So here am I, and I like it. For once I believe I have reached my goal or that is to say, I have found what I want and want to do. I like my work very much and the people are wonderful. It is so different from Charity and the people in that hell hole of New Orleans. I would have rotted if I had stayed on down there. Believe me I am almost like a new fellow.

In that same letter, he says,

> I hope Mary Beth's health is fine and that you have twin
> boys this time. If you need an accomplished obstetrician call
> me. Incidentally in the middle of the above, I went down the
> hall to the delivery room and delivered the second of a set of
> red-haired twins. One a boy and one a girl. They sure were
> cute. I also got in on three sections (Caesarian) so far and
> have done one whole operation by myself.

My father met my mother a few days later. Her date book bears
a notation on August 19, 1943, simply, "met Stokes." Mother had
graduated from the University of Texas with a degree in sociology
in the spring of 1943 and moved to Dallas. With most of the male
social workers away in the war, she was able to get a job with the
local social services department, even without the usual training.
She had a room in a boardinghouse run by Mrs. Karner and took
her evening meals at Papa's house. O. L. Wilkirson, her paternal
grandfather, whom she called Papa, lived in a big red brick house
on Swiss Avenue with Searce, his second wife, and his youngest
child, Ida Moss. His first wife, my great-grandmother, died when
Ida Moss was still small.

Mother remembers meeting my father but didn't think much about
him one way or another. Her cousin Jim Johnson was in medical
school at Southwestern where Daddy was teaching. One night
when she was spending the night with her friend Lucy, cousin Jim
went looking for her. "He came and found me and said, 'Let's go
get a Coke,' and he had a married couple with him and Malcolm.
So Lucy and I went with them down somewhere to get a coke.
Malcolm went in and played the pinball machine in this place, and
they took us back and that was that."

A few days later, Daddy went looking for the shy beauty with the
dark hair. As was frequently the case with him, he only had about
half the information he needed, but he never let a little thing like
not knowing where he was going stop him. Mother tells it this way.

> Sunday night, Mother and Daddy were there, we were at
> Papa and Searce's. Papa lived on Swiss Avenue, and Ms.

Karner's sister was married to a very wealthy man who lived down there on Swiss. And Ms. Erwin her mother lived with the sister. Well, the sister went away in the summer. So Mrs. Karner and I were over there with her mother in this huge house. The master bedroom had an air conditioner in it, a window unit. It was an enormous room with a fireplace and sitting area. So Ms. Karner and I were living it up in the air conditioning. But I was down there at Papa's. And so Malcolm came to where Mrs. Karner was.

He was asking for Mary Jeanette Hooks. [Hooks was her Aunt Jeanette's last name.] Ms. Karner knew the whole family, so she told him where I was, and he came driving up down there in his convertible.

I did remember his name. I was proud of myself. That was all. Papa and Searce, Mother and Daddy, I don't know who all was there.

My father heard Papa call my mother by a nickname, Netta; everyone else had always used her given name, Mary Jeanette. From that day, Netta was what he called her.

On September 25 Daddy wrote to Henry about his zest for life,

> ...there are certain parts of my spirit which I hope will never grow up. I want to always feel young as I do now and I always want to enjoy the moonlight and the dance and things that maybe you thnk [sic] are a little too earthy.

He lived life fast and demanded everything it had to offer. He never gave up loving the moonlight, feeling young, or earthy pleasures. His approach got him into trouble and caused other people more than a little pain, but it was his way. Twenty years after he wrote those words, he would leave my sweet, reliable mother for a much younger, earthier woman. But that's getting ahead of the story.

In the September 25 letter to his brother, he mentioned my mother.

> I guess Mother told you about the little girl they met.
> Well, I have given her up as she had a boy friend out in

the Pacific and I don't know, I just couldn't stand going on with nothing to go on, and I would soon have gottne [*sic*] in so deep that I never could have pulled out.

I'm not sure my mother actually had a boyfriend in the Pacific. She had been dating several men during her senior year of college; most of them had gone off to war. She was corresponding with several of them, and, if attempting to deflect my father's advances, it might have been convenient to mention one of them.

On October 3, my father writes,

I went back to see that little girl after writing you last time. She is still mighty sweet but I guess she just wasn't meant for me. As you can see from her pictures she is right pretty.

They had a few dates and my father decided Netta was the one for him. She wasn't so sure. By October 12, he was mad with Mother for being wishy-washy.

Dear Netta,

Did you ever stop to think what it is that makes you say, "I don't know" or "well, maybe", or "I guess so"? Do you realize the cause of your uncertainty?

I am not one to preach to you or to anyone else, because I am so full of fault myself, but, Netta, if you don't sit down and take account of yourself pretty soon you are someday going to wake up and find that you will never be able to think for yourself and be dependent on someone else the rest of your life. And that is no way to be if you will look around you and see.

You are a smart girl with a college education and a good back ground [*sic*]. If you would only use some of those talents which God gave you. Are you content with nothing to work for or strive for; then never to be able to be on your own. If you are then you are making a good start. But if you are not and want to demand respect and have people think a great deal of you besides just for your beauty or your body, then you had better snap out.

This is perhaps a mean letter from one who thinks a great deal of you, but I probably won't be around anymore and you can hate me for this if you want to, but if I can help you to find yourself I will feel that I have accomplished something.

So, goodbye, sweetheart, and may your years and days be filled with happiness and your life a blessing to many.

The next day, the pendulum swung back the other way and she took his pin. I've never understood why. My father's letter is more insulting than convincing. She probably did seem wishy-washy to this young doctor who was determined to succeed in life. She was young and probably not very focused on forging a life. She was just trying to work a job and have a pleasant time. All she ever said about any of this was that she gave in to him to get him to stop badgering her. Later that week, my father wrote his brother about his plans.

October 16, 1943

Well, I've got some news. Netta is wearing my fraternity pin. I am looking for a ring now and so don't be surprised if you hear of my engagement in the next few weeks. I really make enough right now to support a wife, I think. I work 2 1/2 hours a day at North American for 250 a month. So that added to my 175 from here makes a right nice little income. Also I have a few ligitimate [sic] rackets on the side.

Ever the optimist, he concluded,

Say, Old boy, if I should get married in the next couple of months would you be able to come out this far to the wedding? Just a thought.

The note on Mother's date book on October 13 simply says, "Pinned." October 28 says, "Malcolm—gave pin back to him." Daddy bought a ring and gave it to her several times. She'd give it back, and then here he'd come again. This went on for a while.

When Daddy wrote to Henry in November 1943, he was thrilled on two counts. Henry and Mary Beth had a baby boy, Henry Jerome Stokes, III, who would be called Jere, and my father had news of his own.

> Congratulations old boy and I am just about as happy as you are. I would have wired but then I got to thinking I would sit down and write you a real letter instead. What I was going to wire was this "Congratulations tell Henry III that he has a new Aunt to be." Yes, that's right. I will be sending you the date real soon I hope. I have bought a ring and is it a beauty. Netta hasn't taken it yet because she's still too flustered but she has said yes and as soon as her feet hit the ground again we will begin to line things up. I think it will be sometime next February. I guess I have gone a little fast but then things like that hit me and I know what I want and work toward that end.
>
> I sure am happy for you that you got a boy and I know you are too. I guess Mary Beth did OK as they usually get along pretty well after a couple of babies. Tell her hey for me and how proud I am to be an uncle again.

Mother says my father always wanted a son. His enthusiasm over Henry's son is evident in this letter. Since I was my father's oldest and only child for many years, I had some sense that he would have been happier if I had been a boy, or at least a tomboy. He could have had so much fun playing baseball, riding horses, and playing golf with a boy. I was terrible at ball games, terrified of horses, and his attempts to teach me to play golf ended in his exasperation and my tears. He persisted in his desire to have a son until he finally got one, years later in his second marriage.

Daddy was jumping the gun on the marriage thing, as was his tendency. He had bought a ring, pried one tentative yes out of her, and was already trying to set a date. Over the following months, he would give her the ring in flowers and in candy and she'd give it back. She says,

We started dating. He just took over. He gave me a ring, an engagement ring, I think it was Thanksgiving, an engagement ring, and I gave it back to him. I didn't want it. And this went on and on. So finally in the spring, Mother [MamaMay] said, "Well you've got to do something."

She says he wore her down and she said yes to get him to stop pestering her. Not the best reason to agree to marry someone, but Mother always tried to be agreeable and defuse tense situations. At twenty-one and a half, I'm not sure she knew what she wanted. My father was there when most of the men she knew were off at war. He was cute, and he was a doctor.

In the early spring of 1944, Daddy wrote to Henry,

> About the wedding I don't know a d— thing. The papa is still on outs with me so I can't say anything yet. Netta had her tonsils out yesterday up here and has gone home for a week to recuperate and will try to make some plans while she is there. I hope so. If she doesn't hurry up I am going to get tired of waiting and join the army.

Mother's parents were not enthusiastic about my father as a potential son-in-law. My father looked like a flash in the pan to these hard-working, responsible, small-town citizens. He was charming, but they were not swayed by charm. They spotted him as a man who was moving too fast, who had set his sights way up high.

Mother's parents knew about making commitments and sticking to them, not just for years but for generations. They were land-owning people, whose ancestors sold land in places like North Carolina and Tennessee to buy land in Arkansas and Texas. They were farmers and ranchers, who kept an eye on the value of what we call capital. They were careful, conservative, and self-protective, generous with those they loved and suspicious of anyone who might try to take away anything they had.

I'm sure they feared he might swoop in, steal their daughter, and take her to a bad end. They were at least half right. After he married her, he took her to Oklahoma, and there she stayed. But they were also wrong. She did not belong to them, and in marrying my father, she succeeded in getting away from an extended family that was so large and held sway over so much physical and psychological territory that it threatened to suffocate my shy, polite, rule-following mother. She was never sorry that she moved to Tulsa. I never once heard her say she missed her family in Texas. She liked the bright, shiny, new life in the "Oil Capital of the World," as Tulsa was known in those days. She enjoyed the houses, country clubs, and even the airplane my father bought, though she would have been horrified to know that he was always over-extended financially.

By Saturday, April 15, everything had been worked out for my parents' wedding, but nothing was easy. Silver and china patterns were hard to get during the war, so Mother selected from what was available. Henry's wife Mary Beth got a chicken bone lodged in her throat, which prevented her from attending the wedding. My father writes:

> Say, I was indeed disturbed to hear about Mary Beth's trouble with the chicken bone....

> Yes, we have finally got the go-ahead signal from the father and are scurrying around....

> Netta has decided on French Renaissance silver and hasn't yet picked out her china. Her family is giveing [*sic*] her all the silver, etc. She bought her wedding dress to-day and a lot of her clothes.

> We went to the ice-capades the other night and it was one of the best shows I have ever seen. Boy, it was really smooth.

> It is just five weeks from to-night when the big event is to take place. Gee.... We plan to go down to the gulf coast on our honeymoon. It ought to be pretty down there in May.

Mother and Daddy got married at the First Presbyterian Church, Itasca, Texas on May 20, 1944, a day that was so hot people still talk about it. Mother's family attended the church in Itasca because the tiny Presbyterian church in Grandview had closed. Many of Mother's relatives lived in Itasca, which meant she saw lots of her cousins in church on Sundays.

The wedding reception was held across the street from the church at her Aunt Jeanette's house. Mother's cousin Charlotte was the maid of honor and Daddy's brother Henry was the best man. My father's parents, Henry and Viola Stokes, came all the way from Savannah for the occasion. In the pictures, Viola looks like a normal person in her hat and proper Sunday dress. She wasn't.

Mother and Daddy took off in my father's car for a honeymoon in Gulfport, Mississippi, and New Orleans. Mother had only been out of Texas twice, once to New Mexico and once to Louisiana. My father wanted to show his new bride the beautiful Gulf Coast and the exotic city where he had lived. They didn't get very far, however, before Daddy was giving Mother fits—he wouldn't stop to let her go to the bathroom. I can just hear him, "Oh you're young, you can hold it." It almost sounds like a joke now, but Mother knew then that she was in serious trouble. When Malcolm had his mind set on something, getting him to adjust or cooperate would be nearly impossible.

I've always wondered how the rest of the honeymoon went, especially since that was the only story Mother ever told about it.

* * *

Before they got married, Daddy lived at the hospital, which provided rooms for the interns and residents and even laundry service. After they were married, Mother and Daddy lived in an apartment in Dallas, "a real nice apartment," as my mother put it. It was hard to get a nice apartment in 1944 unless you knew somebody, and though Mother was related to half of Texas, she didn't find the apartment; my father did. In August 29, 1944, Daddy wrote to Henry and said, "I stay at the hospital so much now that it is almost like I am not married.... Netta hates cooking so we eat out most of the time."

I find that amusing, since my mother later became a good cook. By the time I was in high school, she was taking French cooking lessons, buying only the freshest meats and vegetables, using Mediterranean herbs, and producing elaborate, delicious meals.

When my parents got married in 1944, Mother says she thought my father would set up a practice in Dallas and they would settle there, but becoming a doctor was probably the last thing Daddy did that anyone expected.

* * *

My father began to hear about Tulsa from doctors in Dallas who knew an administrator at Hillcrest Hospital. The city was on its way to becoming the oil capital of the world and was growing fast. The hospital needed and was recruiting doctors.

Daddy also heard about Tulsa from a Dallas neighbor. Solly (as the man was called) was a salesman who traveled to Tulsa regularly to call on McDonnell Douglas, the aircraft manufacturer, known simply as "Douglas" then. The two young men played golf together all the time, and Solly mentioned how great the courses were in Tulsa. Since Daddy liked the sound of that, Solly and his wife took Mother and Daddy to Tulsa to look around.

My father wrote his brother Henry from Tulsa's Mayo Hotel ("Six Hundred Rooms Each With Bath"), saying he and Mother "came up here with some friends to spend the weekend and see a little of Oklahoma. We are going to the O.U. football game tonight and are having fun just like on our honeymoon, staying in hotels, etc."

My father and a fellow ob/gyn resident in Dallas decided to move to Tulsa and open a practice together, but the other guy, Bill Eller, was not quite finished with his training. So Daddy arranged to work with a doctor in Tulsa until the friend arrived. Mother and Daddy moved to Tulsa in October 1945 and rented a third-floor apartment in the Boulder Park Apartments at Main and 18th Street. Bill Eller arrived a few months later and he and Daddy bought a little house on 15th Street and opened the "Clinic of Gynecology & Obstetrics."

When Dr. Eller moved away a couple of years later, Bill Henderson took his place. That partnership lasted until the early 1950s, when the U.S. got involved in the Korean War and the government started drafting doctors and dentists who hadn't served in World War II. Mother says,

> They decided that all these doctors and dentists, who were able to practice, could practice medicine in the service. So every time I went to a dentist, he got called up. It got to be funny. So, first Bill Henderson had to go, then Malcolm had to go.

Ten
On the Day I Was Born
1951

My dad was cheering for me from the very beginning. First, he got my mother pregnant. It was a project he worked on for six years, at home and at his office. As an obstetrician and gynecologist, he must have read journal articles and consulted with his colleagues. He delivered babies all the time, but for six years, he could not produce one of his own. Finally he decided to try a procedure affectionately known as "blowing out your tubes." A doctor inserted dye into the fallopian tubes and then took pictures to see if the tubes were blocked. For some unknown reason, the procedure increased the chance of getting pregnant immediately afterward. It worked. Mother got pregnant with me.

Not only did my father get my mother pregnant, he was in the delivery room when I was born. At a time when other fathers were relegated to a waiting room down the hall, he was allowed to be present.

The doctors (my father and his partner) set my mother's due date as May 20, 1951, a fortuitous day since it was my parent's seventh anniversary. The day, a Sunday, came and went with no birth. My mother turned 29 the following Friday, May 25, and still no baby. Daddy grew impatient. He was to play in a golf tournament the following week and wanted to get the show on the road, so on Saturday he decided they had waited around long enough.

The way Mother tells it, Daddy called on Saturday, May 26, and said he was sending his partner, Bill Henderson, to pick her up, that they were going to have the baby that afternoon. The Oklahoma State Amateur (golf tournament) was on Monday, and he didn't want to miss it. Mother agreed. When they arrived at St. John's Hospital, they parked in the doctors' parking lot and that's when Dr. Henderson thought to ask her, "Did you eat lunch?" "Yes," Mother answered, "I had a peanut butter sandwich." He said, "Oh, dear. I don't know whether we can do this. If you have to have anesthesia, you might get sick at your stomach and throw up." He meant she could throw up, strangle, and die. It happens. You aren't supposed to eat if you are about to have a baby, but no one had told my mother.

So she sat there, half in and half out of the car, very pregnant, while Daddy and Dr. Henderson figured out what to do. Finally they decided they would chance it, took her up to the delivery room, prepped her, started a continuous caudal (a spinal anesthesia), and induced labor. She was there all afternoon and was awake. She says there wasn't anyone else laboring in the delivery room that day, and the nurses were all very nice to her. She got the shakes when they said she was about to have the baby, so they gave her a shot of something, and she went to sleep for a while.

Meanwhile they had let my father in the room. He was running around taking pictures but had forgotten to put film in the camera. "Thank goodness," Mother exclaimed at the thought of this. She wasn't crazy about having her picture taken even when fully clothed.

I was born at 7:25 that evening. Mother says she never felt any pain, except her back hurt afterward from lying on the delivery table, and the peanut butter sandwich stayed down. When they were wheeling her out of the delivery room, Daddy presented her with a channel-set diamond bracelet.

Once I was born, my father continued to monitor my progress. He stopped a nurse from feeding me a bottle, insisting I be breastfed. Mother complied. If someone would just tell her the rules, she was glad to follow them. I'm not sure what my father knew about breast milk at the time, but subsequent research has certainly shown that it's better for most babies.

Back out in the parking lot that afternoon or evening, some creep stole my father's golf clubs out of his trunk. People took all kinds of things out of the doctors' cars, usually looking for drugs. When Daddy discovered they were missing, he called the newspaper and asked them to run a notice saying that while his baby daughter was being born, his clubs were stolen, that he needed them back, and that he wouldn't press charges. Sure enough by Sunday evening, the golf clubs appeared under a bush in front of our house. My family was fond of saying that I appeared on the sports page before I appeared on the society page.

That time, my father got everything he wanted: a baby, a story in the paper, his clubs, and the tournament on Monday. I was never completely sure which one pleased him the most.

Eleven
Leaving Day
1952

When I was small, I thought Oklahoma and Texas were the center of the universe, a perspective my Texas relatives encouraged, I'm sure. That may be why I thought Georgia was stuck off in some dark corner of the Deep South. It surprised me, as an adult, to discover that my father's hometown of Savannah had long been a cosmopolitan city. Located on a good river at the edge of the continent, it was a center for international commerce and a doorway to the world. Before airplanes, people and goods crisscrossed America on trains and traveled around the world by ship.

I wonder whether growing up in that port city fed my father's desire to travel. As a boy on the beach at Tybee Island, he could have looked out at the sea and longed to cross it. On the docks at Savannah, he would have seen ships from far-off places: New England, Europe, even Africa. A person could get on a ship in Savannah and go all the way to Tahiti, which might have fanned a boy's desire to see the world.

My father wanted to go places and see things. One of my cousins remembers that when he'd come to visit, he'd always say, "Come on, Sugar, let's go…." Fill in the blank: to town, to the beach, to get some ice cream. He just liked to go.

When he got the chance, Daddy did not hesitate to leave Georgia for parts unknown, first for North Carolina and college at Duke, later for New Orleans, Dallas, and eventually Tulsa.

The first time my father left our home for any length of time, I was fourteen months old. It was 1952, and he was drafted into the

United States Air Force for two years during the Korean War. He was thirty-four and was leaving a well-established medical practice in Tulsa.

I recently came across some pictures of Daddy dressed in his Air Force uniform. His khaki pants and long-sleeved shirt are not yet straining over his small, squat, compact body. A flat-top service cap with a bill sits jauntily on his head. It must have been the day he left for basic training in Alabama. Everyone looks cheerful in the pictures taken in the backyard of our house on Trenton Avenue. They must have assumed he was headed someplace safe to deliver babies and not into armed conflict. It was summer, and Mother's graceful legs are visible below her short red shorts. In some of the pictures Daddy is holding me, and in others I'm with the African American woman who worked for us. (Mother can't remember her name, and I was too young to know.) MamaMay (my mother's mother) must have been visiting and is visible in some of the pictures, as is Hank, our Dalmatian.

A white picket fence is visible at the back of the yard. Mother has often mentioned handing me over the fence to tall Mrs. Bearden, who lived behind us. I have a physical memory of being lifted high in the air and passed from one reliable pair of female hands to another. Mother was never possessive and was willing to leave me with any number of friends, relatives, and young women. I had scores of babysitters, mostly nursing students from a Tulsa hospital. Over time, I developed strong opinions about which ones were good at playing with me and which ones were not.

The pictures have faded. In one small, square color print, only the red of my mother's shorts shows any color. Everything else is in shades of sepia. In another picture, dated July 5, Daddy is squatting in front of me, with his left hand on the brim of his hat and his right hand in his lap. I have my right hand resting on his knee and my left arm sticking straight out beside me, for balance. I am just over a year old and am wearing a light-colored sleeveless pinafore with big ruffles at the shoulders. As I gaze up at my father, he smiles back at me. We appear to be totally enthralled. The blazing sun casts dark shadows beneath us and washes out part of my brown hair.

After several months in training in Alabama, my father would go on to Long Island to begin his service at Mitchell Air Force Base and to find a house for us to live in. It would be almost six months before I'd see him again. Mother says he was supposed to come back to Tulsa for a social event, but he couldn't get away. She went to Alabama at least once to see him that summer, and he was going to join us in Texas at Christmas, but the weather was bad, and he couldn't come. I have no memory of his absence, but then I have no clear memories from before I was two.

There is nothing unique in being without my father for long stretches of time. It is an experience shared by hundreds of thousands of American children whose fathers were shipped off during World War II, Korea, Vietnam, or the most recent conflagrations in Afghanistan and Iraq. I suspect it made these fathers special, because we couldn't have them all the time. In my case, it began the pattern of his being away.

* * *

After Daddy left that summer, Mother and I went to Texas for a while, and then her younger brother Oscar Lee drove us back to Tulsa. We stayed in our house in Tulsa that fall while Mother did her Junior League provisional work. She had to be in town to fulfill various requirements in order to become a full member of that volunteer organization. Just before Christmas, Mother packed everything up in the house. Yes, everything—furniture, dishes, clothes, toys—and shipped it to New York. Then Oscar Lee drove back to Tulsa and took us to Texas for the holidays. In January, Mother and I flew to New York where my father had found us a house on Long Island.

Mother says, "We were supposed to go one day, but Malcolm called and said the ice and snow was so bad that we shouldn't come." So we went another day in January. She felt okay about flying because she had flown back and forth from Tulsa to Dallas several times. Having a toddler with her on the long flight was something of a problem, especially since she had not reserved a seat for me. We sat next to a nice man and woman who had some connection to the Madame Alexander doll company. (My relatives had already started giving me dolls from that company, and they would become my favorites.) The couple offered to move so Mother could get me off her lap. I think they went to the area in the back of the plane where passengers could sit at tables and play cards. Can you imagine such a thing today?

Daddy had found a house in Levittown, a new "planned community" famous for its uniform streets and houses. One house would have a garage on the left, the house next door would have one on the right, and so on down the block. Many of our neighbors had moved out from New York City and were thrilled to have detached houses and yards. Mother found the house cramped and the neighbors, well, different.

My father's assignment in New York was to deliver babies for the Air Force. Mother remembers, "Those women up there at Mitchell Air Force Base were just elated." They were thrilled to have a well-trained ob/gyn.

She was happy, however, to have lots of babysitters available. She says, "I had all those women around there who liked to babysit, and we'd run into New York City. I had a good time up there." They traveled some to Bermuda, and to New Hampshire for a golf tournament.

I think my father had more fun in the service than a lot of people. In addition to using his medical skills, he was able to play a lot of golf, and he took my mother into New York City frequently to go to nightclubs and Broadway shows. When my cousin Beth came to visit from Georgia, she complained that she never saw her uncle. He was always on the go.

* * *

The Air Force seemed to think it was great that my father was such a good golfer and let him fly on Military Air Transport Service (MATS) planes to play in civilian tournaments. The military encouraged golf as a morale booster, and various branches sponsored their own tournaments. He went to Seattle for the U.S.

Amateur and to England in the summer of 1953 to play in the British Amateur.

Mother remembers that Daddy wanted to go back to Britain the following year and wanted to take her with him. The April 1954 USGA *Journal and Turf Management* notes that "Although this is the bicentennial of the Royal and Ancient Golf Club of St. Andrews, Scotland, the United States participation in the British Amateur apparently will be on a somewhat lesser scale than in recent years." About twenty had indicated they would be playing at Muirfield, Scotland, the last week of May, among them Dr. E. Malcolm Stokes, of Garden City, NY. The magazine says some of the players would continue on to the French Amateur, at Saint-Germain, the first week of June.

My parents were to be gone for six weeks, so MamaMay and Granddad drove to New York to take me back to Texas with them. I was about to turn three. When my grandmother arrived at our house and I announced that I wanted to have a *buth-day pawdie*, she nearly fainted, wondering, "What have they done to my grandchild?" I had lived on Long Island for eighteen months and learned to speak the local dialect.

When my parents left for Europe, Daddy took the train to Washington and got a MATS flight to Paris, while Mother took a commercial flight from LaGuardia, the airport in New York. When Mother's flight landed at Gander, Newfoundland, she was confused. "I looked at a clock in Gander, in the big metal building, the 'so-called airport,' and it was thirty minutes different from New York time."

From Gander, her plane flew to Glasgow, Scotland, where she and the other passengers had breakfast before flying on to London. My parents had arranged to stay in London near Cookie, a golfer my father had met the year before. So Mother got a cab and went straight to Kensington Close, the apartment hotel where Cookie lived, checked in, and waited for my father to arrive from Paris. Looking back, she's amazed at herself, "1954, thirty-two years old, just traveling around the world."

While in London, Mother and Daddy got to see England's young queen, once riding in her carriage and once waving from a balcony at Buckingham Palace. Elizabeth II had been crowned the year before, in June 1953, when she was twenty-seven. Elizabeth and Philip had just returned from a six-month Commonwealth tour, which was the queen's first voyage on the royal yacht Britannia and the first time an English monarch had circumnavigated the globe.

The bed in my parents' London hotel was too soft, and Mother says her back went out. Being a resourceful American, Daddy dragged the mattress off the bed and onto the floor. The next morning, the maid saw Mother lying on the floor and asked, "Madame, where would you like your tea?" Mother laughed as she told me she replied, "Right here on the floor."

That was life with my father—travel, adventure, and surprises for everyone.

Cookie was going to the British Open and offered to take Mother and Daddy to Edinburgh with him in his Jaguar. Cookie's car had bucket seats in the front, which were more comfortable for Mother's back, though she found it unsettling to sit on the left without a steering wheel. My father sat in the back and Cookie drove.

There was no apparent speed limit on the two-lane roads, and Mother recalls, "We'd just go zipping along. Every now and then we'd have a race with somebody in another car." With no plan about where to spend the night, they just drove along. When they came upon a 300-year-old inn, Cookie suggested they stop for drinks. The place had rooms available, so that's where they spent the night. Mother was amazed by the age of the place and thought, "This is a *300-year-old inn* and I'm from Texas. That's older than the United States."

The next day, they motored on. When Cookie saw one of his golfing buddies, they stopped at a golf course, right on the North Sea, and played golf. It was May and not very warm in Scotland. While the men braved a cold wind off the sea, Mother took refuge by a fire in the caretaker's small cottage. She remembers thinking that whatever was burning in the fireplace didn't look like wood and decided they must be burning peat.

The trio finally arrived at Muirfield, the course where the tournament would be held, and Cookie dropped Mother and Daddy off at Greywalls, their hotel. While in Bermuda earlier that year, my father had met a golfer from Scotland who said that Greywalls was right on the golf course and was the best place to stay. So that's where they stayed, right by the clubhouse, with all the "big wigs," as Mother calls them. A grand structure right at the edge of the North Sea, the Greywalls Country House Hotel had once been a private home. Mother says it was lovely. Their room was large, with feather beds and a private bath, and a maid brought tea in the morning. The food was so good that Cookie wanted to come over and eat every meal with them.

Being right next to the clubhouse turned out to be a great benefit. Since Muirfield was a *Royal and Ancient* golf club, women were not allowed in the clubhouse, except maybe once a year when they were invited for dinner. (Even then the women had to come in through a side entrance, eat with their husbands, and leave.) Tents had been set up for the women, but it was cold and the wind blew all the time, and the American women weren't very happy with the arrangement. Even in her wool skirt, cashmere sweater, and coat, Mother was cold, so she enjoyed taking some of the other American women to her hotel next door, for warmth or tea.

Mother had her thirty-second birthday while they were in Scotland, so to celebrate she and my father went into Edinburgh for dinner and the theater. She doesn't remember the show, only that someone came by her seat selling chocolates and other treats. They toured Edinburgh and its palace with "all those steps." Cookie ran up the steps, which convinced Mother he was a real athlete. At the top of the stairs, the guard by the gate was wearing a kilt, and Cookie dared her, "Ask him what he wears under it." Mother just laughed.

Cookie took them to a factory that made cashmere sweaters, where Mother bought sweater sets for herself and several friends. The short-sleeved shells and matching sweaters were all the rage in 1954. She bought me a kilt and kept looking for fabric for herself.

She owned a lightweight wool suit of Scottish fabric that she dearly loved and hoped to buy some similar fabric. Someone finally explained that the fabric she liked was made especially for export. People in Scotland needed heavier wools to keep warm.

Cookie paid for everything while they were in England and Scotland. The English were limited in the amount of money they could take out of the country, so Daddy would simply pay him back when they all got to Paris, giving Cookie some cash to spend.

After the tournament was over, Mother and Daddy rode the train across Scotland to Glasgow. There they caught a plane to Copenhagen, where it was warmer. My southern parents had been having a hard time with the chilly weather. In Copenhagen, the unusual sights included jams of bicycles at traffic lights and women in sidewalk cafes smoking big fat cigars. Before going to Paris, they made a brief visit to Brussels where Mother bought lace; they visited Waterloo and were astonished by acres and acres of greenhouses where grapes were grown.

Meanwhile, Cookie had gotten his car across the English Channel and somehow met my parents in Paris. Mother and Daddy couldn't get into the hotel they had reserved, because the previous guests wouldn't leave, so they went to another hotel on the Rue de la Paix near the Ritz, one some friends had recommended. The hotel was gorgeous and comfortable, but, as late arrivals, they had a different room each day. One room was small and had no bath at all, while another was large and lavish with gold fixtures in its private bath. While Daddy and Cookie went off to the golf course, Mother stayed close to the hotel for the daily room change. She amused herself by walking around the neighborhood, admiring the flowers in the Tuileries, and having her hair done in Elizabeth Arden's at the Ritz.

They saw the Eiffel Tower and the tourist sites by day, and at night they went to places like the Moulin Rouge for the follies or "nude shows," as Mother called them. At the first of these, Mother was startled when all of a sudden some women walked out on stage with hats on and no clothes, well, almost no clothes. My father loved it.

One evening they drove out from Paris to a restaurant Mother's sister-in-law had said they should visit and be sure to order the wild strawberries. Cookie knew about the place, so they all went. Mother loved the teeny strawberries served with heavy cream. She said they were no bigger than the end of her finger and had a flavor like none she had ever tasted. On the way back into Paris, Cookie, the Englishman, got on the wrong side of the road and had to veer off the road to avoid killing them all. "That Cookie," she says, "he was a character."

When it was time to go home, Daddy took Mother to the airport in Paris, and then he went off to get a MATS plane back to the U.S.

* * *

Daddy was due to get out of the service right after their trip. Once they were back on Long Island, the movers came and packed them up, and Mother and Daddy got in the Cadillac convertible and drove away. They stopped in the Midwest to see the friends from Dallas who had first taken them to Tulsa. From there, they went on to Tulsa and down to Texas, where I was. Mother was wondering, "Do you suppose Jeanette will remember me, it's been six weeks." As she tells it, I was asleep in a bedroom at my grandmother's, and when Mother walked in the room, I woke up, stood up, and said, "My Mommy!"

That year it was so hot in Texas and Oklahoma that even seasoned residents were complaining. There was no air conditioning in any of our relatives' houses or in their cars. Daddy went back to Tulsa alone to receive the furniture, shipped from New York courtesy of the United States Air Force, and to get our house ready. He stayed in the Bliss Hotel and was grateful for the window unit in his room. People were begging to get into air-conditioned hotel rooms, and Daddy's friend who owned the hotel kept saying, "Malcolm, can't you get that house ready?"

Mother remembers it as a summer of horrible heat and the worst part was that the cars were so hot. When our house was finally ready, Mother packed me into the car and left Grandview at 5:00 on a sultry morning. It was so hot that she wouldn't even let herself stop at an air-conditioned restaurant, for fear she'd never leave it. When we finally got to Tulsa, she was thrilled to have a house with working air conditioning.

The heat continued, but that Fourth of July, my father played in a golf tournament in Tulsa anyway. He was from Georgia—what was a little heat to him? But this was a different kind of heat. The ground was so hot, it literally blistered the bottom of his feet.

Scorching heat or not, we were home. All three of us.

Twelve
Learning to Fly
1954

By the time we moved back to Tulsa in the summer of 1954, my father was determined to learn to fly. Once something like that got his attention, there was no stopping him. He took flying lessons at a local airfield, got a license, and bought a Cessna 180, a sturdy little plane that could hold four adults and me. First produced in 1953, the single-engine 180 was a workhorse of an airplane, a favorite of bush pilots flying in remote places like Alaska and Africa.

As a child, I was susceptible to motion sickness. Riding in the car to the grocery store could make me queasy, and flying usually made me sick. On one flight back from Texas, my father was in the pilot's seat, and I was lying in the backseat with my head in Mother's lap and my hands in a new white muff my grandmother had just given me. I remember saying, "I have to spit up," but the plane was so noisy that Mother couldn't really hear me and thought I said, "I have to *sit* up." So she sat me up, and I threw up all over myself and the fluffy muff. Over the years, I became proficient at managing those little white bags on airplanes.

I didn't think my father's being a pilot was unusual. He was just my dad. He was a doctor, just like some of my friends' fathers. He flew off to places like Japan. But I had one friend whose parents traveled to places like India to visit hospitals on behalf of the Presbyterian Church. How was I supposed to know what was ordinary and what wasn't?

I guess I felt the way a kid might feel if her dad drove a taxi. Flying was a way to get around. I was accustomed to being taken places—

to Texas, to New York, back to Texas—in cars, commercial planes, and then my father's plane.

In December of 1955, when I was four, Daddy flew us to Georgia for the marriage of my oldest cousin Gail. The wedding was in late December, and my parents had decided to make a winter holiday of it. They were planning to leave me with relatives and go on to the Caribbean with their friends the Blisses, who came in the plane with us. When bad weather forced us to land in Memphis for the night, Mr. Bliss, a Tulsa hotel owner, got us rooms at the Peabody.

A grand hotel built in the 1920s, the Peabody has a two-story lobby with an elaborate fountain with live ducks. I don't remember the ducks from that first visit, but I do remember the enormous lobby. Fifty years later, when I stopped at the hotel on my way from North Carolina to Oklahoma, I walked into the lobby, looked up, and knew I had been there before. To a small child, it was like staying in a castle. When we finally arrived in Macon, I got to be a princess, or at least the flower girl in Gail's wedding.

When my friend Sally Patton moved to Houston in the middle of elementary school, it was convenient that my father had a plane. He flew Mother and me to Houston for a visit; and another time he picked Sally up, and we all went somewhere together. Flying in a little plane was a big deal to Sally. To me it wasn't anything special; it was just one more trip in the upchuck machine.

I thought of my life and circumstances as normal and was mostly unaware of difference based on race or class. The children in my school all seemed about the same, except that some were smarter and others could draw. They were white, and nobody was dirt poor. My father wanted us to live in a house befitting a successful doctor. By the time I started school, we lived in a four-bedroom house in which I had a whole wing and a playroom all to myself. My friend Amy, who shared her house with four sisters, must have thought ours was palatial.

The next house had a swimming pool, which didn't strike me as terribly unusual. Given the heat in Oklahoma, everyone I knew either had a pool or had access to one. Years later, a childhood friend reminded me that my family was the first among our friends to have a swimming pool as well as the first to have a color TV.

About the time the plane, the swimming pool, and the travel might have translated into status for me, my parents got a divorce. Mother and I moved into a two-bedroom apartment, where we lived in fewer square feet than any of my friends. The apartment was new and nice, but it certainly wasn't what I was used to. Mother gave me the larger of the two bedrooms, which meant I was mostly able to avoid feeling I had stepped down a notch from being *the doctor's daughter*.

I might have caught on that something was unusual when Mother didn't get a job after she and Daddy were divorced. She said my father and grandfather were helping us, which was true, but I didn't understand that being able to pay for an apartment and buy food and clothes without having a job made you rich by definition. We only lived in the apartment for a year before she married my stepfather and we moved into yet another nice house. Back in 1955, I thought flying around in my father's airplane was as normal as riding in a Chevrolet.

Thirteen
Grandmother's Funeral
1957

Two years after I was the flower girl, we flew to Georgia again. I had turned six in May, my father turned forty in June, and in July his mother had a stroke. The photograph of all of us on the beach at Tybee Island has "August 1957" written on the back. Uncle Henry's diary notes that on August 8, 1957, "Malcolm, Netta & Jeanette flew in from Tulsa to see Mother. Cessna 180." Mother recalls that we stayed at an old hotel in Savannah and that we went to the beach. Never big on antiques, she simply thought of Savannah's prized DeSoto Hotel as "old." I have almost no memories but do have a few photographs from that trip. I especially like one on the beach where I'm making an exasperated face. Like my father, if I wasn't having fun, I wanted something to change immediately.

Back in Tulsa that September, I entered the first grade. A couple hundred miles to the east, the Governor of Arkansas and the President of the United States were duking it out over the integration of Little Rock's Central High School, but I was oblivious to the drama. My teacher, Mrs. Terhune, was a kind woman who easily communicated her love for learning and her affection for children. My only struggle was with the door of the building, which was too heavy for me to open with ease. I had no idea that police officers in the next state over were actually blocking the school doors to nine black students.

When Grandmother Stokes died in October, Mother and Daddy got in the Cessna 180 and headed for Georgia. Henry's Sunday diary reads,

October 6, 1957

Weather perfect.

Mother died at home, 301 West 37th Street, Savannah, Georgia at 9:45 AM, peacefully & quietly.

Mary Beth, Jerome, Sharon, & I got off for Savannah to be with Dad at 11 AM. [Two men] took over the AM services. [Two relatives] went into Savannah immediately to be there until we arrived at 3 PM.

Malcolm & Netta flew to Macon & spent night in our house. Talked to Beth at Oberlin at 10 PM. She wanted to come for funeral, but distance was too great.

Recently, I noticed that I have no memories of that funeral, so I called my mother and asked if I had been there. "Oh, no, we didn't take you," she said. "We had Elizabeth, and you were in school." Elizabeth was the older, white live-in housekeeper we had for a few years in Tulsa. Mother said she didn't think I needed to go again, since we had just been to Savannah a few months before.

That was the first of many family funerals I missed. I didn't attend Grandmother Stokes' funeral in 1957 or Granddaddy Stokes' funeral in 1971. I'm even confused about where my grandfather's took place. He died in Oklahoma, where he had been living with my father, but he's buried in Georgia. In any case, I wasn't there. I didn't fly to Texas for my beloved MamaMay's funeral in June of 1974. And, as I've said, I didn't attend my father's funeral in 1976. It was almost an accident that I was present for my Texas grandfather's funeral in 1965. He died at Christmastime while Mother and I were visiting.

When I added all this up, I began to wonder why I had missed so many family funerals. Mother and Daddy didn't take me to Grandmother Stokes' funeral, and Mother didn't encourage me to show up when other relatives died. The pattern puzzles me, especially since I am now so willing to attend funerals.

Mother and I had a strange conversation after her mother-in-law Thelma, my stepfather's mother, died. Mother was in the hospital room when Thelma died, and I think it was the only time she ever witnessed anyone's last breath. When she called to tell me Thelma was gone, I thought she might be shaken by the whole experience and asked how she was doing. (I'm the minister, right?) She said it was sad but that it was fine. I was not particularly close to Thelma but asked if Mother wanted me to come to Tulsa for the funeral. She answered that I was welcome to come if I wanted, and then said, "I know you would like for me to need you like that, but I don't."

What? Had I heard her right? I felt slightly disoriented and was having trouble getting enough air. I heard myself say, "OK. Let me know how it goes."

That exchange has stayed with me for decades, and I've wondered who it was she didn't need. I could be wrong, but I don't think I was asking her to need me. Was that pronouncement meant for someone else? For *her* mother? She was fairly independent and had pretty much avoided needing other people. Her words could have been a pledge of self-sufficiency made years earlier, a vow to do things on her own: tie her shoes, brush her hair, or get her homework right without anyone's help. Mother could follow the rules and even accomplish tasks she disliked, such as sewing, well enough to get an "A" and to be the valedictorian of her small high school graduating class. To this day, she cleans her kitchen to perfection after each and every meal.

I can understand that she might not have needed my presence at funerals, especially since I'm the emotional one. I might have upset her, and she never liked to feel upset. The problem on my side was that when my father died, I needed *her*. And when my beloved grandmother died, I might have liked a little encouragement to come to Texas and be with the family. She had too much family growing up, including two-dozen cousins, most within twenty miles. Once she was grown, she showed up for family events more out of obligation than affection. I, on the other hand, grew up hundreds of miles from any of my extended family. She took me to Texas to stay with my grandmother every year until I was twelve, so she made sure I was well attached to my Texas relatives. Maybe she didn't like funerals or didn't think they were very important. Grief wasn't an emotion that interested my mother very much, or the other women in her family. When my father left, for instance, and she figured out he really wasn't coming back, she wanted to get over it as quickly as possible and move on.

When her own father died in 1965, Mother and I were in Texas for Christmas. My parents were already divorced, so it was just the two of us staying with my grandparents, at their house. My grandfather got sick and was taken to the hospital, with a bleeding stomach, as I recall. When he died on the second day of January, we were still there.

I have a clear memory of sitting on the sofa with my grandmother, in the house she had shared with my grandfather for over forty-five years. MamaMay was between Mother and me, and she was crying. At one point she said, "I don't know why I'm crying. When my father died, our mother didn't cry. She was strong and comforted all of us." I was only fourteen, but it seemed to me that it was completely normal to cry when your life-long partner had just died.

My great-grandmother didn't cry when her husband of almost sixty years died. My grandmother didn't think she *should* cry when her husband of fifty years died. My mother didn't like to cry, period, and would later report that she wasn't upset when her own mother died. She's the one who never encouraged me to show up for funerals. In more recent years, I have failed to attend the funerals of a Georgia aunt and uncle, a Texas aunt and uncle, and a Texas cousin (a first cousin, not a distant one.) For two of those Texas funerals, I was already visiting in Tulsa and could have arranged to attend. But I didn't, and saying that makes me feel like a bad person. When I search inside myself, what I find is an odd feeling of disconnection.

I began learning to ignore loss and sadness in the fall of 1957 when my parents left me in Tulsa and went to Georgia to bury Grandmother Stokes. My elders practiced stuffing their grief deep below the surface, and I honed that skill when my father left. Though his departure was the worst thing that had ever happened to me, I tried to follow their lead and keep going as though everything was fine. Just as poor circulation produces cold fingers and toes, shutting off some of my feelings left parts of me slightly numb.

Fourteen
Around the World
1957

Grandmother Stokes died in October of 1957, and two months later my father left on a trip around the world. I was six, and I remember he was gone for a really long time. When he finally returned, he brought movies, gifts for Mother, and dolls for me.

My father carried a movie camera on this trip, and I grew up watching images of him standing in front of the Kremlin in Moscow and all bundled up in Kabul, Afghanistan. When I recently asked my mother about the camera, she said she knew exactly what it was. She purchased a 16 mm Bolex for my father in May or June of 1951, right after I was born, so he could take movies of me.

The H-16 Deluxe Bolex camera came out in 1950, weighed five and a half pounds, and had a strap across the top to make it easier to handle. I think Daddy let me hold the camera by the strap, or try to. I can still feel the heft of it in my hands. He lugged that thing in its special case all the way around the world and then showed his movies to anyone who would watch.

As a child, I spent many an hour in our darkened living room with my parents and others, transfixed as I watched our lives or my father's travels moving silently across the screen. Daddy usually narrated from the back of the room, speaking loudly to be heard over the whirring projector next to him. Sometimes he'd walk up to the screen and point at something with his finger, blocking out the rest of the action with the shadow of his body.

Of all the home movies I watched as a child, the images that are clearest to me are of my father in Russia. Wearing a heavy wool coat and stomping his feet on Red Square, he'd wave to us and point to the Kremlin in the background. Those images made his trip real to me.

Sometime after I became an adult, I realized the movies had disappeared and felt sick every time I thought about them. Though Mother still had lots of footage of me, Daddy must have taken the movies of his trip when he moved out. We should have thought to ask someone about them when my father died, but I never even met his third wife, and Mother wasn't about to get in the middle of it. If only someone had thought to give them to a library.

My father's friend Hal Matheny cooked up the trip around the world because he wanted to go to Russia. A pilot with American Airlines, Hal loved to travel. He and his wife Pixie (the swimmer) had taken a trip around the world a few years before, but they didn't go to Russia. Hal had always wanted to go Russia, but when it finally looked like it might be possible, Pixie didn't want to go. Then my father said he'd go. Hal did all the work to get the trip organized, and Daddy got to go along.

American travel to Russia had been severely restricted for decades, but then things began to change. Stalin died in 1953, Khrushchev denounced Stalinism in his "Secret Speech" in 1956 and took control of the government in 1957, and the cold relationship between Russia and the U.S. thawed briefly. (The Cuban Missile Crisis was only four years away.) The Russians and the U.S. State Department began to allow American tourists into Russia, and Hal wanted to go. He was adventurous and so was my father. As Mother said, "Malcolm was game for anything." Daddy told her she could meet them in India, but she wasn't interested in flying to India by herself.

As Mother recalls, "They left in the winter, November, and went to Finland and then to Russia, and *that* was exciting and scary. And then they flew down to Tashkent, in the Uzbek Republic; the people there are mostly Muslims. I think that is when they saw one of the original copies of the Koran. And from there they flew to Kabul."

It still amazes me that they went. Joseph McCarthy died in the summer of 1957, and Americans were only beginning to get over being afraid their neighbors were "Reds" (Communist spies). When I asked Mother if she was nervous about my father's traveling "behind the Iron Curtain," she said she didn't think so. Once they got it all worked out and had the visas and reservations, she wasn't worried. She said, "I was kind of used to him doing far-out things. He'd say, 'There's a golf tournament in Seattle,' and off he'd go. No, I don't think I was too concerned. I had been to Europe, and Hal and Pixie had been around the world. It was OK. The State Department wouldn't have let them go if it was dangerous."

It wasn't a simple trip. Hal had some trouble getting permission to go to Russia and had to work at it. There were restrictions on where they could travel. To get to the places he wanted to visit, Hal had to cobble together pieces of three government "tours." Once he and Daddy arrived, they were constantly in the care of a special guide and suspected their hotel rooms were bugged. (Scholars tell me that their rooms were surely bugged and that every tour guide was KGB-approved.)

Daddy left Tulsa just before Thanksgiving and went first to New York. He wrote to Mother from the Hotel Belmont Plaza, which advertised itself on its stationery, "Lexington Ave., 49th to 50th Sts., New York. On New York's fashionable East Side. You can walk to shops, theaters, night clubs, Radio City, U.N. and all the gay mid-town area. 800 outside rooms with tub and shower bath. Many air conditioned. Television available." He reports, "Nice flight up to N.Y. No trouble yet," and instructs her, "Cut my picture out if it ever comes." I assume he's referring to the newspaper. Daddy loved to have his picture in the paper and to send clippings to his relatives in Georgia. He also instructed her, "Take the keys out of my Jaguar & lock the trunk. (Medical bag.)" Remember, his golf clubs were stolen when I was born. "Hug Jeanette for me. All my love, Happy Thanksgiving! Malcolm." Thanksgiving was November 28 that year.

From New York, Daddy flew to Sweden, where he met Hal. In a letter from Stockholm on Hotel Malmen stationery, my father reports a struggle with his travel clock.

Leaving for Helsinki today. Just had a funny experience.
We went all around trying to get someone to fix that clock
the office crew gave me and finally found a man who told
us what was wrong. You have to wind it up!! Ha! Brilliant
Americans.

He continues.

As normal Hal and I ate a big good meal at an elegant
restaurant last nite. Had a good floorshow, too.

Bought some pretty crystal & shipped it today. Hope it gets
there OK. Some of the stuff I buy will be gifts but you can
open it all & we can sort it out when I get back.

Hug Jeanette.

Mother says, "He bought nice things, had most of them shipped
home, I guess. It was a big, big adventure." For over fifty years, my
mother has been pointing to objects in her home and saying, "That
little dish is from our trip to Copenhagen, or your father bought
that in Thailand when he went around the world."

What Mother remembers of Hal and Daddy's visit to Finland is
that he bought glass vases and he had a sauna. She says, "That was
the first time I had ever known about that. Go out and roll you
in the snow and beat you with birch branches." His postcard of
November 27, 1957 from Helsenfors (Helsinki) reads,

Still going strong. Sure is cold. Bought some fur-lined
shoes. Had a Finish Suana [sic] yesterday. (Like a Turkish
Bath.) Soaked out all the Scotch. We're invited to a party
in Moscow at the Ambassadors on the 30th. Hope you
are well. Bought some pretty things for you! Hal is a fine
traveling companion. (But I miss you!!!!) No girls yet
(just soap.) I want you! Etc. Leave today at 3 o'clock for
Leningrad. Talked to some people who just got back &
they say it is cold! 10 [degrees] here so if it's colder, we will
stay indoors.

My parents had been married for thirteen years by then, and I find
my father's comment, "no girls, just soap," to be both risqué and

endearing. Perhaps he had teased her ahead of time about the sexy Scandinavian women. It would have been just like him, and after *Casablanca* (1942), every American man on holiday in Scandinavia expected a young Ingrid Bergman to knock on his hotel door.

I'm sorry that I have no cards or letters from Russia, because Mother says that was the most exciting and the scariest part of the trip. It was also the part that Daddy talked about the most and the film footage he showed the most often. When he got back, people in Tulsa were eager to have him show the movies, and he seemed happy to share his stories with anyone who would listen.

Mother saw the images over and over. She says, "The movies, which we don't have, were very interesting. Nobody in Tulsa had been to Russia. He showed those movies to one organization after another. They were really good. All kinds of people were calling him, particularly people interested in Russia and Afghanistan. Nobody we knew had ever been to Afghanistan. The whole thing— Burma and Thailand. If you asked me I'd probably say, 'Yeah, I've been to Afghanistan.' I saw them so much."

There is even a note in Uncle Henry's diary on Friday, March 21, 1958, saying that Daddy came to Macon and showed the movies of Russia.

> Malcolm and Netta arrived from Tulsa in the Cessna 180. Flying to Miami for a cruise with friends. He showed pictures of trip around world and Russia to [eight men listed].

The local newspaper, the *Tulsa World*, carried three stories about my father's trip to Russia. On January 15, 1958 there were pictures of my father with a Moscow boy, Hal with three young men in Tashkent, and a dreary government building in Leningrad. The article described some of their adventure.

> The Hal-and-Mal team spent two weeks in Russia as paying "guests" of the government's Intourist Bureau. For the privilege of traveling behind the Iron Curtain, with an almost ever-present interpreter, they paid $30 per day each.

Theirs was the *de luxe* tour. They rode the subway in Leningrad (a subway with no rest rooms in the stations), went through a women's hospital, visited a textile mill, a shoe factory, a circus, a movie, a puppet show, a collective farm, a ballet, a museum, a TV studio—and a second-hand store.

The Leningrad State Women's Hospital, naturally enough, fascinated Dr. Stokes, the obstetrician. "The women work seven and a half months of their pregnancy, then they take off six weeks," he said. "After they have the baby, they have six more weeks to nurse it before they go back to work.

"During the six weeks of 'vacation' before delivery, they have four two-hour lessons on how to relax and have a baby. No anesthetic is used at delivery. The 'lessons' seem to be a form of do-it-yourself hypnosis.

"The doctors answered the questions I put to them through our interpreter. I found out later that the interpreter had been up most of the night studying a medical dictionary to be able to use the correct terms in relaying questions and answers!"

Abnormal delivery cases are granted local anesthetics, Dr. Stokes was told. Instruments were far from modern.

"We saw one male doctor," he said. In fact all through the Soviet Union, the continuing question was: Where are the men? They never got an answer.

Matheny said the Russian transportation "always left on time. You could easily be left behind. Five minutes before a plane was supposed to leave, its doors were locked and if you were late, you waited for the next one. The same was true of the trains."

The travelers did not keep the same interpreter throughout their tour. When they boarded a plane or train, they were left to their own devices, or in care of the transport officials who frequently spoke only Russian or their own language, of which there are some 125 in the Soviet Union.

"If we were weathered-in anywhere, and that did happen, we couldn't count on an interpreter being around. But one time we were 24 hours late and when we landed we found the poor Intourist man—a new bridegroom—had been waiting all that time for us," said Dr. Stokes.

Commerce was difficult. In the stores that supposedly sold new items, everything was "sold out." Daddy told the reporter about trying to sell a suit at a second-hand store, but they offered him too little money and too much red tape.

Hal discussed the ins and outs of flying with some of the Aeroflot pilots and discovered he was allowed to log many more hours than they were. But the Russians seemed most amazed by the fact that my father owned his own plane. "This was so obviously American imperialistic capitalistic propaganda that there wasn't any use discussing it," my father laughed as he told the newspaper reporter.

Mother had said the buildings in Russia were beautiful and that Daddy's movies of the Kremlin and the churches were gorgeous. The church is St. Basil's; I'm sure you've seen pictures of it. It's the one built in the sixteenth century with the brightly colored domes on top. When I closed my eyes, I could see Daddy standing in front of St. Basil's church, wearing a brown hatbox shaped hat with furry earflaps that could be tied up or pulled down over his ears. But the movies were gone, and the newspaper articles picture him in the hat but not in front of the church. I remember being fascinated by the hat when he brought it home. It was so much heavier than any hat I had ever seen. I had never been anywhere cold enough to inspire the creation of such a hat.

When Hal and Daddy were waylaid on their flight from Moscow to Tashkent, they got nervous. Mother remembers, "The weather got bad or something and they had to land, and of course they put them in this little hut or something, and they were there until the plane could take off again. It was a Russian plane they were flying in." I imagine they spent some hours wondering whether this was the first stop on the way to a Siberian work camp.

From Tashkent Hal and Daddy flew to Kabul, Afghanistan, where cold and snow delayed them for four days. They stayed in a hotel, but there wasn't anyone to help tourists, and they had trouble finding anyone who could speak English. Mother recalls that Hal the pilot thought, "There's got to be somebody in the tower at the airport who speaks English." They did find a young man who worked at the airport, spoke English, and agreed to be their guide in Kabul. Later on, that same young man came to visit us in Tulsa.

Mother says there was only one paved road in Kabul, built by the Russians, but otherwise the streets were dirt. She remembers seeing animals up on the sidewalks in my father's movies. In one of its articles about the trip, the Tulsa paper reported that the Afghans wouldn't let the camel caravans use the paved street, "They make 'em go up on the sidewalks." The Americans were building a dam up in the mountains, but the people in Kabul seemed much more interested in the paved road and a bread factory the Russians had also built. My father described Kabul in a letter to my mother.

> Kabul
> December 10, 1957
>
> Dearest Netta,
>
> It is snowing outside and I doubt if we leave today as scheduled. Only 1 plane to Delhi in the past 2 weeks. We had a gorgeous day yesterday & got a lot of nice pictures. We met this Afgan [sic] fellow who is coming to Okla City to study. Anyway we hired a taxi to go to a small town 25 km away & the taxi (a Russian made auto) had a flat & we had to walk halfway back. Finally hitched a ride on the back of a rock truck & then got to the edge of town & caught a horse & carriage. What an experience.... Then we went shopping in the Bizzar [sic] awhile. The streets are literally seas of mud. Boy oh boy. Then last nite this fellow invited us to his home.... What a feast! Sitting around on the floor [with your feet] under the table—warmed by a brazier under the table & every kind of dish imaginable. It

was quite an experience. I gave him my yellow scarf & he gave me a goat skin vest, hand embroidered. Our rooms here aren't too bad. We have a suite for $4 a day with a houseboy who comes in the morning & lights the fire for our bath and in the sitting room.

The King of Afganistan [*sic*] is flying to Karachi Pakistan today. Maybe we can hitch a ride with him. I would hate to have to stay here for 10 days like some of the people ahead of us have. Fortunately we have one of the 3 bathrooms in the hotel.

Hal says tell you hello & we miss you. The only female face we have seen was a girl at the Embassy office. The other women all wear these things on their head. Even the boys home last nite we… never saw any women at all. His father has 3 wives & is living in NY with the youngest.

The women in Afghanistan were covered by *burqas*, and my father bought a child-size for me. It was brown and silky, and when I put it on, it covered me from head to toe. Wearing it was such an unusual experience that I can still close my eyes and remember how it felt to have it on. There was a woven screen through which I could see, but I remember feeling totally hidden.

His letter continues,

Hal has the K.T. (Kabul trots) again. Sure hope he doesn't run out of medicine. Fortunately I haven't had it yet. Maybe we can get a new supply of medicine for him in India.

Don't believe we will go to Indonesia due to the trouble there. May get to come home early. Already homesick for you!! Probably have trouble getting reservation anywhere with the Dutch fleeing the Far East. Wish I heard from you in Delhi.

Love, Malcolm

India was the next stop. Daddy sent Mother a postcard on Friday, December 13, 1957 with a picture on it of the Taj

Mahal. The caption reads, "Taj Mahal, Agra. The world famous mausoleum built by Emperor Shah Jahan in memory of his wife Mumtaz Mahal between 1630 & 1648 A.D." He sent it to my grandmother's in Texas with the barest hint of an address:

Mrs. E. M. Stokes
C/o Mrs. C. T. Wilkirson
Grandview Texas
USA

There were only 1,000 people in the town, but it still amazes me that it arrived. The card read,

> We finally got one out of Kabul!!! Boy, what a place. We have had 2 really interesting weeks. Now we feel like we are back in Paris. A very swanky hotel. Your letters were the high point of the trip!! Driving to Agra today. We lost a day in Kabul so having fun trying to catch up on our schedule. Sure wish you would meet me in Hawaii.

> Love, Malcolm

Daddy sent me a Christmas card from India, with a picture on it of two Indian women carrying jugs on their heads. The inscription reads, "TO GREET YOU AND WISH YOU A HAPPY CHRISTMAS AND A BRIGHT NEW YEAR." Inside he wrote,

> Jeanette,

> Have a big Xmas and Daddy misses you very much. He will have a pack full of surprises for you and we will look at my pictures and have a lot of fun together. I hope Santa Claus was real good to you. Hug and kiss your Mommy and Mama Mae [sic] for me.

> I love you
> Your Daddy

He made good on his promise and brought me lots of presents. He must have bought me a doll in every country he visited, because I eventually had three long shelves of them in my bedroom. The ones

I still have fifty years later remind me that when my young father was traveling far away, he still had me in mind.

By December 16, 1957, my father and Hal were in Burma, and Daddy wrote to Mother from the Strand Hotel that day.

Dearest Netta,

I just scared the daylights out of Hal! I went out to change some money on the black market and didn't get back for 45 minutes and when I came back he was like an old mother hen that had lost her "biddies". He was running around like a chicken with its neck chopped. And to top it all I didn't get the money. Went through Chinatown (Rangoon) so you can imagine where I was. I couldn't have found my way out with a road map. And the odor & incense & people. Fortunately I got back all in one piece and now the d. fool has gone to try to do it himself. Ha! He said to call the embassy if he wasn't back in 15 minutes. You see, the official rate is 4.70 to 1 & Bl Mkt [Black Market] is 9 to 1. So we can cut our expenses way down & get some pretty pretties with the difference.

I'll let you know if Hal doesn't get back.

We saw a lot of Pagodas today. We are up to our ears in museums, churches, pagodas & history. I will have to come home & study to find out where I have been.

Have fun in Texas. I miss you & love you.

Malcolm
Squeeze Jeanette for me!

A postscript notes that Hal finally got back an hour and half later and that by then, Daddy was the mad one.

In Rangoon, Burma, my father bought small gemstones. I have a square-ish gold pinky ring that Mother or I had made with some of the stones. I can't wear it, which makes me think it was originally made for my mother's thinner fingers, but I love holding it and rubbing my finger across the raised stones fastened to a wide gold band.

Daddy mailed another postcard to Mother from Burma. This one, dated December 16, 1957, pictures a streetscape in Rangoon.

Dear Netta,

I didn't get a letter here & was so disappointed. Hope to in Bangkok. Still going strong but homesick. This is a beautiful place. People are very friendly. Hope you are having fun & I miss you.

Love
Malcolm

The next day, still in Rangoon, he sent a postcard to his office that pictures Burmese dancers who look just like Thai dancers to me.

Dear Folks,

Think I ought to stay here awhile? The climate is wonderful. People friendly. Can't speak English. Having a good time. Anyway [*sic*] I go from here I start toward home. Oh boy! Hope you are well.

Yours,
Dr M

From Burma the travelers flew to Bangkok, Thailand, where Daddy bought lots of bronze items for the dinner table. Later on, I remember eating off bronze forks, which tasted funny and were probably a lot of trouble to keep polished. Mother explains, "Hal and Pixie had been around the world a year or so before, and they bought all that bronze flatware: knives, forks, spoons, plates, bowls, everything. Malcolm bought a bunch of that, I guess he had it shipped, and fabric, because after the war an American stayed there and had a business of all that Thai silk." For years I had a big piece of pink Thai silk with gold embroidery on it. Mother says she had a red and pink plaid silk two-piece dress as well as some other garments made of the fabric my father brought home.

The only correspondence I have from the final days of the trip is Daddy's postcard to Mother from Hong Kong. It shows a picture of the harbor and the caption reads, "Scenery of Aberdeen Harbour the fishing junks sailing, with the floating restaurant in the distant view." I remember those restaurants, because Mother, Daddy, and I ate in one of them a few years later. Dated December 22, the card reads,

> We skipped Bali, Singapore, [unreadable]. Had lunch today at the restaurant [pictured on the card]. Very picturesque. Having a good time. Very very homesick for you. Bought a lot of pearls perfume silk, etc. Hope to give you your Xmas in January. My love to your folks. I hope to be home Jan 4.

> Malcolm

Mother remembers, "All of a sudden Malcolm decided he had to get home, got on a plane, and he flew all the way from Hong Kong or Tokyo to Dallas. Hal told him not to do it, but he did it." He got to Dallas on New Year's Day and what he most wanted to show us was a silly tongue scraper he had in his pocket. That would be my father. Even bleary-eyed, his sense of humor was still intact.

I always thought of my father as a great adventurer with minimal ties to home, but I see from these notes that I was wrong. He writes with the same love, enthusiasm, and longing for connection that he expressed to his brother when he was younger. Later when he left us, I wanted to believe it was because he wasn't very connected to either one of us. Somehow that made the loss seem smaller. I've accused him of only being attracted to my mother's beauty and to me because he wanted a child, any child, but now I think I may have been wrong. His leaving doesn't mean he never loved me. Still, thinking that he loved me and left anyway is almost more than I can bear.

I will never completely understand my parents' relationship. All I know is that a distance grew between them, and it wasn't one I could fill. Children are not glue, though God knows I wanted to be. For all the years since my parents split up, some part of me has been trying to put the pieces back together, to restore the family that came apart, to make sense of the new people who entered my family—halves, steps, and the ones I wanted to ask, "How are you related to me?"

Fifteen
Holidays
1959

The year I was in the third grade, my father decided to build a house with a pool. It was a great house to live in and a perfect house for parties. When we returned from Long Island five years earlier, he had bought a long low stone house on a huge lot and planned to sell the front yard to someone else and to build a house for us in the backyard. The plan worked. One family built a house in front of us, and Daddy sold the existing house to another family. We moved into a rental while our new house with a swimming pool was being built of cinder block and lots of glass. The living room would have terrazzo floors and be so large that my parents could push back the nine-foot sofas, roll up the rug, and have a dance party—which was my father's goal.

While our new modern house was under construction, we rented an old-fashioned, two-story house nearby. I loved the big old house with its basement, where my friends and I practiced tornado drills, and its dark staircase, which I descended like a queen to her subjects below.

I got sick the fall we lived in the rented house. Well, first I got tired. I had so little energy that I couldn't practice my leading role in the school's annual play. When I invited playmates over after school, I'd lie down on the bed and Mother would have to send the children home. Finally, when I was too tired to go to school at all, Daddy or another doctor ran some blood tests. Sometime after that, Mother and Daddy sat me up on the kitchen counter and explained that I had the beginnings of rheumatic fever (a strep infection that had spread to my bloodstream). I'd have to stay in the bed for a while, but they assured me a good drug would cure me. I took up residence in a hospital bed in a large bedroom on the second floor. My father appeared with a hypodermic full of penicillin and gave me a shot in my butt, which hurt so much that I wondered whether he was any good at his job. Regular shots of penicillin and blood draws left me needle-phobic, and to this day, I warn nurses to write "hates needles" in big letters on the front of my medical chart.

It was December when they clapped me in bed and not long before Christmas, so Mother asked what sort of tree I might like and offered to put it in my room. "A pink flocked tree!" I pleaded. Can you imagine? So that's what we had: a fluffy tree, with fake pink snow, in my bedroom, for weeks and weeks. Teachers came to see me, even my elementary school principal. Family friends brought me an edible gingerbread house, and children sang carols outside my window. Once I stopped being so tired, I found it all pretty entertaining. A "home-bound teacher" came for an hour once a week, though it was surprising that a mere hour at home was equivalent to a whole week at school.

In a photograph from this period, I am sitting up in a high bed by the window, wearing a paper cone-shaped party hat, waving a stick with short streamers, and blowing a noisemaker. It must have been New Year's Eve, and my father, who loved holidays, or Mother, who was trying to entertain me, thought of party favors. I look like I'm having fun.

I loved holidays. I'm not sure if it was because I was an only child and was often the focus of holidays, or because I was sick that one winter and got so much attention, but I loved holidays—Christmas, New Year's Eve, Halloween, and most of all birthdays.

Mother and I spent months planning my birthday parties. Some years I produced hand-made invitations, such as the ones for a swimming party, which I decorated by drawing sprays of blue water. That year, Mother had a bakery put a big blue pool and tiny plastic bathers on the cake. At my "Backward Birthday Party," the children wore their clothes backward and came in the back door. The living room furniture was turned around backward, and we had cake before lunch.

I liked planning the parties, getting the children to play my games, and opening presents. I was rarely disappointed by presents on birthdays and Christmas, because Mother often asked what I wanted. My parents, grandparents, and Santa frequently came through with just what I had in mind.

As an adult, I've been surprised that so many people hate holidays, ignore their birthdays, and dread Christmas. I cock my head and look at them as if to say, "Don't you recognize a good thing when you see it?" I've known people who even ignored their fiftieth birthday. They must not know that people will do almost anything you want for your fiftieth birthday! A few reluctant men even danced at the rock-and-roll party I threw for mine.

Perhaps I caught my love of holidays from my father, who loved celebrations of every kind. His role at birthday parties was to tease the children and take pictures. Trick-or-treating was new to Mother and Daddy the first year they were in Tulsa, but Daddy got into the swing by giving quarters to the children who knocked on their apartment door. Word got around and lots of children came by. Later, when we lived in a house, he got Mother to peel grapes and put them in a big bowl, so he could ask the trick-or-treaters to stick their hands in the "eyeballs."

My mother understood her role as full-time wife and parent to include facilitating many of the things Daddy and I wanted to do, so she spent lots of time creating or attending social events. A perfect hostess, she made sure her guests were warmly welcomed, fed and watered, and well entertained. Though she says she enjoyed getting dressed up and going to parties with my father, she hated the part at the end when my drunk father would insist on driving home. I was grown before I realized she was an introvert and might have been just as happy to stay home. Now she and my stepfather have quiet holidays together.

Mother and I spent lots of time in our house when I was young. My father, on the other hand, seemed only to pass through. It was not uncommon for him to be gone when I went to bed at night and gone again when I got up in the morning. He had early rounds at the hospital, got calls in the night to deliver babies, and at other times was out having fun. He'd play a round of golf in the late afternoon and stay for a drink at "the nineteenth hole." In the evening, he'd play poker with his buddies or take my mother to a social gathering. He was frequently gone.

Except on holidays. Maybe that's why I came to love holidays so much: my father was more likely to be around. One Christmas morning when I was about five, we had opened presents, and my father was putting together a large gift for me—a pretend stove or refrigerator for a child-sized kitchen—when the phone rang. It rang all the time and was often for the obstetrician. This time, however, when Mother said the phone was for him, Daddy said he would call the person back. My heart leapt. My father *always* took calls and then frequently ran off somewhere. But not that Christmas morning. That morning doing something for *me*, his only child, was more important than anything else. Anything.

Somewhere along the way, I began to expect holidays to provide something special, something that other days of the year did not. My father was likely to be present, and I could have both my parents in the same place for a while. Somehow, I loaded too much freight onto these special days, and it took decades for me to figure out that I didn't have to try to squeeze everything I needed out of holidays, that love and attention might be available on other days as well.

* * *

I got over the rheumatic fever and went back to school in February of 1960, just in time for my class to load me up with valentines and red heart-shaped boxes of candy. Then the house my parents were building was finished, and we moved in that May.

The outside walls of the new house were cinderblock. Someone must have thought they were modern, and they certainly were sturdy and cheap, but they were ugly. Only one wall in my bedroom was cinderblock, and it was painted robin's egg blue, like the rest of the room. Mother let me pick out the curtains of lavender lilacs for the high window, and I loved the room. It had a built-in desk, two large closets, and shelves for my dolls.

Everything in the house was state-of-the-art for 1960. The kitchen had a blender base built right into the endless expanse of white Formica countertop. The shag carpeting in the master bedroom was made of red, black, and gray loops, and Mother's high heels would get caught in the loops.

The L-shaped house had a swimming pool in the crook of the L with a gallery, a patio, and a waterfall flowing over lava rocks. My father didn't want to fish leaves out of the pool, so he had the whole thing enclosed like a screened porch. It kept the pool clean, but if an adult took a good bounce on the diving board, the person could touch the metal trusses that held up the screen roof. I was always afraid someone was going to hit his or her head.

* * *

I had turned nine the same month we moved into the house, and Daddy gave me a poodle as a gift and also as a bribe. I had been sucking the two middle fingers on my left hand since I was a small child, and I was still doing it in the third grade. Mother would cringe when she'd walk into my schoolroom and there I'd be, left elbow propped on the desk, fingers in my mouth, using my right hand for the assigned task.

My elders tried any number of ways to get me to give up sucking my fingers. My Texas grandfather offered me a cow in exchange for the habit, but I declined. I didn't want a cow. I finally agreed to trade them for a French poodle, so when we moved into the new house with the pool, Daddy got me a fluffy little white poodle I named Gigi. It's corny to name a French poodle Gigi, but I was enthralled with the 1958 movie by the same name. I'd melt when Louis Jourdan sang of Leslie Caron, "Gigi, am I a fool without a mind or have I merely been too blind to realize? Oh Gigi, why you've been growing up before my very eyes." When Gigi was old enough, my parents bred her, and we had more fluffy puppies, two litters with ten pups in all. I was allowed to keep one apricot female from the second batch and called her Mon Cherie. Mother, who had taken some French in high school, later realized the name should have been the feminine Ma Cherie. But it was too late, the name had stuck, and we called the second poodle Monnie.

I loved having dogs that were more my size. The Great Dane and the dalmatian had been too large for me as a small child, and the dachshund was never very cuddly. The poodles would come running to greet me when I got home from school and would sit on the floor with me when I played with my dolls or did my homework. The poodles were *mine,* and I adored them.

Sixteen
Hawaii and Japan
1961–1962

Sometime after we returned from New York in 1953, my father joined the local Air Guard, properly known as the 125th Squadron of the Oklahoma Air National Guard. The way Mother tells it, the Tulsa unit of the Air Guard needed a doctor and asked Daddy to serve, which he said he'd do if they'd bump his rank up a notch to Lieutenant Colonel. The general in charge was a friend of my father's, so perhaps he negotiated the deal. At any rate, my father's hat got more "scrambled eggs," the insignia of his rank, and the 125th got another doctor to do physicals.

My father's joining the reserves came with a benefit: Daddy could once again fly for free on Military Air Transport Service (MATS) planes. This was particularly exciting because by 1960 the 125th had been designated an air transport squadron and was flying cargo from Oklahoma to places all over the world. With escalating U.S. involvement in Southeast Asia, a lot of the flights went to Japan and then to places like Laos and Vietnam. When my father's schedule allowed, he hopped aboard one of the big C-97 cargo planes and went to Spain, Thailand, Hawaii, or Japan.

The planes weren't particularly comfortable for passengers. They were designed to carry tanks, crates of ammunition, and other supplies. That didn't bother my dad. He could sleep anywhere—in the back of an ambulance, at the theater, even standing up. He never complained about the lack of amenities, he'd just lie down on the floor of the cargo bay and go to sleep.

A reasonable person might plan a two-week trip to Asia, but my father would go for a couple of days, the way you or I might run off to the beach for the weekend. He loved buying stuff to bring home. He had a whole cargo plane at his disposal, so he bought things like big heavy stone lanterns, ceramic outdoor cookers, and lots of Japanese dolls. We all seemed to enjoy the outdoor cooker, known as a hibachi pot. We were the only people I knew who had one of the fat, round, waist-high, ceramic Asian backyard grills. Mother or Daddy would start a fire in the bottom, put food on the grate in the middle, close the lid, and let it cook. The food probably tasted just like it would on a conventional American grill, but it seemed exotic to cook on the hibachi.

My father had become enamored with Asian design on his trip in 1957 that included Thailand, Hong Kong, and Japan. He had installed a small Japanese garden by the front door of the house where we lived and incorporated Japanese elements inside the house. When he built us a new house in 1959, he included several rock gardens outside and a narrow wall at the end of a hall where a long painted scroll would hang. In 1960, when Daddy moved his practice into a new medical building at 21st and Lewis, he added Japanese touches to the décor—paper shoji screens in the waiting room and fake characters on the chart holders outside each exam room, which he made out of black electrical tape.

* * *

In June of 1961, Mother and I were in Grandview visiting her family when my father called to say we were all going to Hawaii. This was just the sort of thing that made life with my father both exciting and exotic, especially while I was oblivious to the darker underside of some of his adventures. The Air Guard was going to take Oklahoma Governor J. Howard Edmondson to Hawaii for the National Governors Association meeting, and Daddy planned to go along. He had already bought commercial tickets for Mother and me from Dallas to Honolulu. Someone drove us to Carter Field, the old airport between Dallas and Fort Worth, and we took off for what Mother still calls "a long weekend in Hawaii."

We went first to Los Angeles, where we had to stop overnight. We arrived in the afternoon, so Mother got a car and took me to Disneyland. It was a ten-year-old's heaven to me, even though we walked until my feet hurt and Mother's new flats rubbed blisters on her heels.

The next day, we flew on to Honolulu. Our fiftieth state had been part of the Union for less than two years and rolled out the red carpet for visitors. Literally. We descended the metal steps from the plane to a long red carpet. Beautiful women in brightly colored dresses draped piles of fresh leis around our necks. For free. Mother said to enjoy it, that I might never get treated like that again.

The weather in Hawaii was perfect, except for brief afternoon showers that drove no one inside except the tourists. Mother and I bought mu'umu'us, loose cotton dresses in floral prints. We toured the island, I learned to do the hula, and we rode on a catamaran, a sailboat that looks like a large platform strapped to a couple of canoes. My clearest memory is of the wide expanse of beach in front of the Hilton Hawaiian Village, the resort where the governors met and where we stayed.

Daddy and I were out walking on the beach at one point when he said, "Look, there's Bud Wilkinson." The Oklahoma University football coach was a much bigger deal than the governor. Wilkinson was as famous as a movie star, at least to people from Oklahoma. I knew who he was, and I didn't even like football.

"Order another one of those drinks with the flower," I urged my father as we sat at the hotel's beachside bar. It was an idyllic moment. I had my father all to myself in one of the most beautiful natural spots on the earth. Daddy obliged, ordered another Mai Tai, and continued to get happily sloshed while I arranged delicate purple orchids in a line on the table in front of me.

I don't know what I was thinking—encouraging my father to drink like that. I wasn't in Hawaii; I was in la-la land. Evening parties, poker nights, and even rounds of golf had always included social drinking for my dad, but it had been getting worse. Sometimes Daddy would roar or simply fall asleep at the dinner table. Mother had started backing out on social engagements at the last minute to avoid arguing about who would drive home at the end of the evening. I hated it so much that I tried not to notice what was happening.

So that afternoon in the bar, I focused on my growing collection of flowers, overlooked my father's inebriation, and enjoyed a "perfect" moment in paradise. I didn't know the Hawaiian drinks were invented to please the tourists or that the resort's beach had been manufactured in the 1950s by blasting and dredging the shoreline, piling up 30,000 cubic yards of sand, and planting palm trees for shade. Understanding none of that, I relished my days in heaven.

* * *

About six months after our trip to Hawaii, Daddy said he wanted to take Mother to Japan. She thought it was a good idea and suggested they take me along. So in February of 1961, Mother arranged for me to be out of school for a couple of weeks, Daddy got all the information on flights, and off we went to the Orient. My father hopped a MATS flight from Oklahoma to Japan and arranged for Mother and me to fly on a commercial plane to San Francisco, where we waited a day or two until we could get on a MATS flight to Honolulu. While we waited, Mother took me to the Japanese Tea Garden at Golden Gate Park. Someone must have told her it was the thing to see. First open to the public in 1894 as part of the California Midwinter International Exposition, the small strolling garden is the oldest Japanese-style garden in the United States. Its rock gardens, bonsai trees, pagodas, and bridges made us all the more excited about going to Japan.

Military families were not allowed to fly on MATS planes in the Continental U.S., but we could overseas. All we had to do was wait our turn. There were no reservations, but we did fly for free. When we boarded a propeller plane in San Francisco, we were startled to see that the seats were turned around backward. When we asked, we learned that facing the back was safer in the event of a crash. It seems that commercial airlines didn't want to suggest that planes might crash, so they made the seats face forward. Must have thought it was better for business.

In Tokyo, we stayed in a drab military hotel, and my travel-weary mother didn't think much of the Orient at first blush. She and I had both expected everything to look like Golden Gate Park. Daddy was disappointed that Mother didn't fall in love with Japan immediately, but things improved. I got lots of attention on the Ginza as I paraded about in my white tennis shoes. Schoolgirls in their dark skirts, white shirts, and dark shoes stared at my feet as they asked politely if they could practice their English.

We went west to Kyoto and stayed in a hotel where futons were spread out on the floor for sleeping and then rolled up and put away during the day. We marveled at the Golden Pavilion. I took pictures and Daddy took movies. We all giggled at the squeaking floors in the "singing palace." Clever builders added bent nails under the floors to squeak in the event of intruders.

Daddy was thrilled with the speed of the fast train we rode north to Nikko and Nara, and he laughed when I got nipped in the butt by a deer at the Nara Deer Park. I had fed a deer just like other tourists were doing, but my deer wasn't happy when I stopped and made that clear when I turned to walk away.

My father's enthusiasm for the Orient was infectious. Everywhere we went, I eagerly bought things, as though trying to take the whole country home. I acquired a child-size kimono that I still have, an obi sash, getas and tabi socks, a brass ornament for my hair, fans to keep and some to give away, and, of course, dolls. I increased the collection my father had started and still treasure several of them as much as anything I own.

Returning from Japan was almost as exciting as being there. I was the only child I knew who had been any place like that, which meant I showed my pictures at school, told stories, and got lots of attention. By the time Suzy Henry and her family went to Japan two years later, I was ready to share the spotlight. I had much bigger worries by then.

I turned eleven the May after we went to Japan and celebrated with a Japanese birthday party. Mother put a coffee table in the dining room with large pillows for my girlfriends to sit on. Carefully dressed in my kimono and obi, I demonstrated the proper use of chopsticks. Mother served a tasty sukiyaki, thinly sliced vegetables and meat served over rice, but my friend Amy Clark had a hard time with the chopsticks. After food went every direction but into Amy's mouth, Mother produced a fork.

For years to come, I reported that traveling was my favorite hobby. I may have even put it on my college application. A spark of desire to see distant lands had flown off my father and ignited my imagination like dry grass. I had a passport and I was ready to go.

Seventeen
Flying Apart
1964

The demise of my parents' marriage is all tangled up for me in the nation's loss of a president.

I walked out of my seventh grade English class on the afternoon of November 22, 1963 to get a drink of water. I was twelve. While I was drinking from the fountain in the hall, a male voice came over the loudspeaker, "We have just received news that the President of the United States has been shot." Less than an hour before, that same hallway had been teeming with life, as hot young bodies pushed and shoved their way to the next class, slamming locker doors and squealing as only early adolescents can. But as I stood alone at the drinking fountain, stunned by the unimaginable, the hallway seemed frighteningly empty. The beige glazed blocks of the wall in front of me were unsympathetic and the green terrazzo floor unyielding.

Later that day, I learned President Kennedy had been shot while riding in an open-top limousine in a motorcade in Dallas, Texas, my Texas, just fifty miles from my beloved grandmother. How could that be? Horrible things weren't supposed to happen in places you could picture. Kennedy was pronounced dead at 1:00 p.m. at Parkland Memorial Hospital, where my father had once been a medical resident. Later on that day, Lee Harvey Oswald was arrested and charged with murder.

That would have been unnerving enough to a budding adolescent girl, but that was only the beginning. Later that fall, my father went on a gambling trip to Las Vegas, met a woman, and fell in love—all unbeknownst to me. I got sick with something minor before

Christmas, so we didn't take our usual December trip to Texas. Daddy flew our gifts down to the relatives and picked up presents for us. I found out years later that he took his new girlfriend along as his "co-pilot." She was, in fact, a licensed pilot, but I'm sure that's not why she was along. My Texas aunt who met Daddy for the gift exchange was horrified when the blond bombshell got out of my father's small plane. I am still amazed at my father's audacity—that he would show up in Texas with his new girlfriend.

By February, Daddy had moved out of the house he built for us, rented an apartment, and moved in with the co-pilot, who would soon become my stepmother. Mother says she finally threw a fit, went over to the apartment, and screamed at my father and his girlfriend. She must have called the woman names, because she says my father responded, "She's no worse than I am."

You would think that I'd have some memory of this, the single largest transition in my life, but I don't. Those months in early 1964 are hazy and formless to me. I remember living in the house with Mother for more than a year after Daddy moved out. Late at night the quiet was interrupted by a crunching sound as the night watchman crossed the gravel courtyard near my bedroom window. He was supposed to keep us safe. I liked the feeling that someone was trying to keep us safe, especially since the grown-ups had let some thief break in and steal my family.

I have an image of the day my father left, of walking into my parents' bedroom at the back of the house, and seeing a suitcase and clothes spread out on their king-size bed, the one in which I had slept many times. In this vision, I question what's going on and Mother explains, "I'm helping your father pack. He's moving out." But when I actually asked Mother about this memory, she said it never happened. She never helped him pack; she was too mad for that.

I must have taken other images of their packing for trips and pasted them over the gaping hole in my life. The most likely scenario is that one day Mother simply announced that he was gone. After that, whenever I saw him, he told me how much he loved me. But he had stripped those words as bare as the coat hangers left swinging in his closet. It would take me decades to remember I had ever had a father's love.

* * *

Meanwhile, I assured everyone I was fine. "Worse things happen to people. I'm fine, really." I had proof that I was all right: I still had my mother, my room in our house, and my dogs. But I wasn't fine, and neither was my mother. She went to the hospital with pains in her chest that turned out to be a stomach disorder. No one in her family had ever been divorced, and being left felt like the worst thing that had ever happened to her. She had every right to fall apart. Never mind that we all agree it worked out better for her in the long run. I went right on trying to act as normal as possible, seeing my friends, participating in a junior high social club, and having crushes on boys.

I turned thirteen in May and went to summer camp with my friend Sally Patton in June. She came to Tulsa from Houston, where she was living at the time, and we rode the bus together to Kanakomo Kamp in Branson, Missouri (way before Branson was famous.) I got off the bus, walked in the nearest bathroom, and threw up. Riding a bus affected me just like flying in a small plane. At the end of the five-week camp term, the Pattons and my mother came to the Ozarks to collect us.

That Thanksgiving, Mother and I joined the Pattons (Sally, her brothers, and their parents) at a ranch they owned near Calico Rock, Arkansas. I had known Sally's parents since I was three when we moved in across the street from them and had always liked them. Once they became part of my safety net, I was bound to them forever. As an adult, whenever I'd go to Tulsa to see Mother, I'd try to see Mr. and Mrs. Patton as well, even after they moved to a retirement community miles away on the edge of town, until they died a few years ago.

The empty hallway of my junior high, the crunch of gravel on a quiet night, the lively warmth of the Pattons' cabin—these are the images that remain from that year, these and the awkward visitor who had once been my dad.

When Mother and I moved out of our house and into an apartment the next summer, she gave the dogs away. She said dogs weren't allowed, but honestly, she had never wanted pets; she just took care of them. I was fourteen, and all I remember is that before camp that summer we lived in a house with two dogs, and after we were in the apartment alone. I never saw Gigi again, but Sally had moved back to Tulsa and Monnie went to live with her. I saw that poodle many times, but something in my heart must have closed. She no longer seemed like mine.

Years later, while helping a friend bury her dog, a beloved pet of sixteen years, I saw the sadness in my friend and wondered what had become of mine. I don't remember missing them at the time, but I now suspect that my grief is wound up in the simple fact that I've never had a pet again.

I was fourteen when we moved into the apartment. Mother dated a couple of other men before settling into a routine with Vol. Sometimes I would find them in the evening sitting in our small study, lights dimmed, upright in straight-back upholstered chairs, with a candle between them. They must have been courting. I found the whole thing a little awkward. No one else's mother had a boyfriend, but Vol seemed all right, if Mother was determined to have one. He was quiet and polite, taller than my father, but not too tall, and handsome like the Shah of Iran. He had a boat on a lake near Tulsa and would take us water skiing, which I enjoyed. I was pretty good on a slalom (both feet in a single ski), and Vol let me coach him on his technique.

Then a year or so later, Mother sat me down and told me that she and Vol were going to get married. I burst into tears. Vol seemed nice enough, but I had put up with about all the loss and change I could stand. She told me years later that she thought I was jealous of Vol. Damn straight I was jealous. I had lost my father, my house, my poodles, and now I was losing my mother to some guy I hardly knew.

Mother said they would get married in July (1966) while I was at summer camp and that she'd move all our things into Vol's house while I was gone. There were some good things about this arrangement. The house was in our old neighborhood, I would have a nice big bedroom, and Mother would continue to be my parent, not Vol. After I got over the initial shock of this news, I made some sort of agreement with myself that I'd try to like my new stepfather and that I'd put up with Bonnie, his six-year-old, who turned out to be pretty cute and not much trouble to me.

Vol's house is a really fine example of 1940s modern—long and low, well built, with thick brick walls, well-proportioned rooms, plenty of windows, and a good traffic pattern. It's a good thing, since my mother and stepfather have now lived there for forty-five years. I moved into the back bedroom, with its generous built-in closet, dressers, and storage cabinets, and lived there for three years, until college. It puzzles me now that I have so little feeling for that room. Though I've spent over a thousand nights in that room, it's mostly just a room to me. Some part of me is insistent that while the house is certainly my mother's house, that bedroom is not my room. Not my house and not my family. My family had disappeared.

We spent our first Christmas as a foursome with Vol's mother, at her condo. We sat at Thelma's heavily carved Spanish Colonial dining table, with pressed linens, beautiful china, and plenty of tasty food. Thelma had a housekeeper who lived with her part-time, but the housekeeper's husband had died the day before, so the person who might have helped with the Christmas meal was gone. The elderly black man who stepped in to save the day was careful about refilling both Vol's and his mother's cocktail glasses. As the meal progressed, the two of them became increasingly intoxicated and I gradually more distressed. In silent horror, I sat up straight in my Sunday clothes and tried to act as though nothing unusual was going on. Had my mother gone from one husband who drank too much to another?

The worst moment came while standing in the driveway outside Thelma's home after the meal. As I opened the backdoor of Vol's Cadillac, I realized in dismay that my mother was going to let my stepfather drive. All the way home, I sat frozen and barely breathing and prayed there would be no other cars on the road. Though we all survived the short trip, I was furious and scared.

Even though I never saw Thelma drunk again, and there was never a repeat of that first Christmas, I spent the next thirty years fearing that there might be. When my own divorce in the late 1990s sent me to Codependents Anonymous, I developed a different strategy. If that first Christmas dinner were repeated today, I'd leave the room, call a cab, and go somewhere else, options not available to me at fifteen.

Eighteen
Disconnection
Late 1960s

While I was in high school, my father went on creating his new family, my mother took care of hers, and I fell in step with the late 1960s, teasing my hair, wearing pastel Pappagallos that fell apart in the first rain storm, and swooning over the Beatles. At least that's how I looked from the outside.

My father and his second wife had one daughter when I was fourteen. Within the next couple of years, Daddy and Faye increased their family with a son and Bessie, a baby chimp. Adopting the chimp was part of an animal behavior experiment at the University of Oklahoma. I'll explain more about that later. For now, trust me that she, the chimp, was part of the family. A year or so later, they had a second daughter.

Occasionally, Daddy would pick me up at Mother's house and take me home with him so I could spend the night. He lived with his new family on a lake about forty-five minutes west of Tulsa. Being around Faye and the children always made me uncomfortable. To make matters worse, my father would drink and fall asleep before dinner was over, leaving me alone with these strangers. I'd be helpful and polite and try to focus on the chimp.

I have three small square snapshots of Daddy and this second family. Sometimes I stare at them, hoping they will tell me something more about the father I lost. In one, Daddy is holding Bessie the chimp; she's just a little thing. It is Christmas time, and the picture looks like it was taken in front of the two-story Christmas tree at Southern Hills, where my father played golf. Faye is wearing a plaid dress and smart black knee-high patent leather boots.

Bessie is perched on Daddy's hip and sports a tiny red Santa
hat and suit. Faye is holding Tim, whose outfit matches Bessie's.
Though the boy and the chimp were both about a year old, he
appears to be twice her size. The older daughter is standing on the
floor between her parents, pretty and shy in her red velvet dress
with a white cat on the front, white tights, and black shoes, and
a red band-o that can barely contain her springy blond curls. She
looks like she's between three and four. Daddy is looking at Bessie.
Faye and the little boy look straight at the camera, and the curly
blond gazes somewhere past the photographer. To this day, when I
look at this picture, something inside me flies apart. The very image
is an affront to my life as I had once known it.

In the next picture, the same five are sitting at a picnic table outside
somewhere, looking just as I remember them. It could be at their
house on the lake near Tulsa, or at Southern Hills. I can see the
metal railing of a swimming pool ladder reflected in the windows.
The photo is dated September 1969, and the children look a bit
older. The girl's hair is longer and the boy is bigger. She would
have been four and a half, and he would have been about eighteen
months old.

Daddy is sitting on the far side of the table with his shirt off. His
hair is buzzed short, just as I remember it. He's holding Bessie, and
she's drinking milk out of a glass. Faye rests on a bench in front of
the table with the boy on her lap. The little blond sits on the table
between her parents, reminding me of the Christmas picture. I want
to stop the action, keep them from going swimming—ridiculous
since it happened forty years ago. Swimming was something my
father shared with me. Why was he doing it with these people?

The third picture is dated April 1970. The youngest child, a
redheaded girl, would have been a year old, and it appears to be
her birthday. In the picture the three children are standing beside
a table with a chocolate cake in front of them. The chimp isn't
present. The birthday girl is standing on a chair and has her left
hand flat down on the top of her cake.

They look like happy children, like real children who have
birthdays, like children I might want to know. But as I stare at the

photograph, I can feel myself backing away. What is it I want to avoid?

When I focus on my discomfort, I can recall other times I have felt the same way. The feelings are similar to the unease I have about not being as close to a godson as I think I should be, or not being of more help to some elderly neighbors than I am. In each of these instances, I feel like a bad person.

Wait! Something is out of whack. My father is the one who left. He went off and created a new family, so why am I the one who feels screwed up? I wonder whether I have long believed that there was something wrong with me for not being happy about his new life.

When I think about my father's other children, I feel guilty. I had completely lost track of them. Wasn't I supposed to feel related to them? I was the older one, wasn't I at least supposed to know where they were? I wasn't sure. The only clear feeling I have is disconnection.

That's an odd feeling for an extrovert like me. I am connected. Ask anyone who knows me. I have lots of friends scattered around the country, and I manage to keep up with them. I even created a job for myself that includes getting people together.

Then I remember the photograph of my father squatting before me on the day he left for the Air Force, the way I gazed into his eyes when I was only a year old. If I close my eyes, I can see that clean-shaven face, warm smile, and the glint in his green eyes. The picture takes me right there, to the carefully fenced backyard of my first home. When I compare that to the feeling of dislocation I had when I visited the house on the lake where he lived with Faye, three children, and a chimp, I can see what I lost. Instead of being the focus of his gaze, I was lost in the crowd. He was often lost in an alcoholic fog. I did not feel like a member of that family. When I was with them, I felt as out of place as a Christmas decoration at a Fourth of July picnic.

I think my discomfort was a byproduct of my parents' divorce. Maybe that's why we call such families "broken." If we weren't individually broken, my family was certainly all broken into pieces. My father, my house, my dogs, and my mother had been scattered about, or so it seemed to me. What I got in return was a stepmother I never took to, half-siblings who looked like her, and a stepfather and his daughter who were certainly tolerable. But none of it was mine. All I really wanted was *my* family.

Divorce was not so common in the 1950s as it is today, but in my particular circle of friends in Tulsa, it seemed like everyone's parents were divorced one way or another. One friend lived with a mother and a stepfather, another had a dad who had been married once before, and by the time I was in high school, my father's friends were divorcing their wives and marrying younger women.

Making sense of so much loss and change is a challenge for children of divorce, for kids who lose parents or siblings, for anyone who survives a childhood trauma, for anyone who survives childhood, period. How to go on if once you lived in paradise and then it disappeared, or left, or you left, or you grew up? It may be harder for those of us who lost our innocence all at once, but life is hard on nearly everyone. It leaves us wounded. We can either decide to live our days running, flying away from our wounded hearts, or we can turn to greet them, befriend ourselves, and begin to heal.

Nineteen
Birth Control
1969

Sometime before I went off to college in the fall of 1969, my father asked me if I wanted birth control. Was it on the phone or in person? I don't recall. All I remember is that the question made me uncomfortable. He said he was sad to see all these "little girls" (he meant young women my age) come in his office pregnant and that he was willing to give me any kind of birth control I wanted to ensure I wouldn't wind up like that. I assured him I wouldn't and changed the subject.

When I did start having sex with my boyfriend, I chose the most readily available form of contraception: prayer. Unable to reconcile my father's straightforward approach with my mother's insistence that I not have sex, I chose not to bother much with birth control. Some months later, I accepted that I was having sex, began insisting on condoms, but continued to feel rather conflicted. The most conservative Christians on my college campus encouraged that feeling.

My first year of college, I occasionally participated in InterVarsity and Campus Crusade, conservative campus Christian organizations. At meetings and retreats, I'd promise Jesus I wouldn't have sex with boys any more, but I never kept that promise very long. When I tried to reason with my conservative Christian friends about sex, they'd thump on their Bibles and quote Scripture. I didn't think Jesus really cared one way or the other, and it irritated me that they wouldn't have a reasonable conversation. Eventually, I grew weary of the right-wingers, noticed that having sex seemed to be a fairly regular part of my life, ignored my mother's advice, and let my father's partner prescribe birth control pills for me.

At Thanksgiving my freshman year, I flew from Massachusetts to Colorado to visit my friend Amy at the University of Colorado. We were then going on to Tulsa together in a few days. While in Boulder, I began to have excruciating pain when I peed and was peeing blood. Scared out of my wits, I called my father. "Have you been getting too much?" he asked when I explained my symptoms. I was shocked. I had not called to talk about anything personal. Couldn't he act like the friendly neighborhood pharmacist? He told me that I had cystitis and that they called it *honeymoonitis* because women often got it on their honeymoons. I'm not sure how he got me a sulfa drug. Perhaps he called a pharmacy in Boulder or maybe he told me to drink loads of water and to go to the drugstore when I got to Tulsa. I was just glad to know I wasn't going to die. I still wonder how I kept all this from my mother when I arrived at her house.

One of the things I missed after my father died was being able to consult him about medical issues. If I could get him on the phone, drunk or sober, he would answer my questions. I've tried to replace him various ways—with a college friend who became a doctor, with another friend whose husband is a doctor—but it's never been the same.

* * *

On one vacation home from college, my mother caught me having sex, well, caught me half-dressed, in my bedroom with my boyfriend. She and my stepfather had been out but came home unexpectedly. We managed to get partially dressed before she opened the door with, "What's going on here?" I have blotted out most of what she said after that, though I do recall her threatening to jerk me out of "that liberal college up in New England."

Meanwhile, my stepfather read the riot act to my boyfriend. He probably didn't care so much about who was having sex with whom, but he was furious with anyone who upset my mother. By the next day, we were all acting as though nothing had happened. I went right on doing what I was doing, but not in her house.

By my senior year, I was on "the pill," and when I took up with a nice man from North Carolina, he was delighted with that arrangement. After graduation, I followed him to North Carolina, where I decided that putting all those hormones in my body was probably not good for me. I still remember the day I announced to my North Carolina boyfriend that birth control pills were not healthy and I was going to stop taking them. I explained that not getting pregnant was a lot of trouble and part of the trouble was going to be his. He wasn't happy but complied. I returned to using condoms, added a diaphragm, and went on that way for years. Then I had a female partner. Then I wanted to get pregnant.

* * *

I heard about women at my college going to New York City to get an abortion, but it never occurred to me that they might be going to someone like my father.

When I imagine my father in his medical office with the Asian decor, I see him in a straight white coat, longer than they wear now, one that comes almost to the knees. I see him smiling and standing near the autoclave, as though he is waiting to have his picture taken. I never imagine him doing anything. Oh, maybe he pauses outside an exam room, file folder in one hand, the other hand on the doorknob, waiting to enter the room, another photo opportunity. But when he opens the door, there is nothing inside. The room is empty, as it might be on a TV set.

The only image I can conjure is of my father catching babies in a delivery room. Everyone is gowned and masked in green cotton cloth. Lots of drapes cover the woman in labor, and when my father comes in, all you can see of him are his glasses and bug eyes. He stands politely next to the woman's feet, which are in stirrups, and catches a fresh clean screaming baby as it slides out all at once.

I have attended two births, neither of which looked anything like what I just described.

When I have gynecological exams, I never imagine the doctor (male or female) as my father, though I tell most physicians my dad was an ob/gyn. The whole process of a gynecological exam is humiliating: taking off your clothes, placing your feet on cold metal supports, shoving your butt in some stranger's face—things your mother told you never to do. (This work should have been left in the hands of women.)

Never have I imagined him getting close enough to smell a woman's private parts. Neither do I want to visualize my parents having sex. Yuck. I know my parents had sex, but I don't want to picture it.

But my father spent his days that way, with women half-clothed, in vulnerable positions, scared, and often feeling powerless. Stripped of their natural authority, they lay on their backs, even to give birth, a position that was mostly for the convenience of the doctor. Don't get me started.

I never got pregnant in college, though I wasn't always careful. I never got pregnant, period. When I tried to get pregnant in my late thirties, it didn't happen. By forty, I was in the early stages of menopause. My theory is that I inherited my mother's reproductive system. She had trouble getting pregnant and went through menopause in her early forties. I don't have any scientific proof, but I say we had low fertility rates.

Twenty
Abortion
1972

My father was arrested for performing an illegal abortion in Oklahoma in 1972. At the time, I was embarrassed. No one in my family (that I knew of) had ever been arrested. Good people didn't get arrested. (Anti-war and anti-nuke protestors were in a different category. They were making bold public statements about injustice.) My father had left my mother because of another woman, and performing an abortion seemed like one more sleazy, secret, possibly immoral, certainly illegal thing he had done. If he had done it. It was never clear, and I didn't ask many questions. It was disconcerting enough that my father spent his days with his hands up women's skirts. I wasn't eager to find out if he did illegal procedures on the side.

What he did tell me was about the time he got beat up. I think it must have been around that same time, when he was living alone, after Faye left and before he got married a third time. One night, he opened the front door to two big guys, who pushed their way inside. They were yelling something like, "You killed my baby," and beat the crap out of him. The whole time, Daddy kept thinking, *Just don't kick me in the head.* He had recently had cataract surgery and a lens implant. The doctor said to avoid quick movements with his head. Being a human punching bag was not on the list of recommended activities. My father either told me about this episode on the phone or in person some months later; I never saw his bruises. He thought the guys were actually hired by organized crime in an effort to scare him. I'm not sure if he told me or if I surmised that he thought the attack was to scare him out of doing abortions. He thought the "you killed my baby" line was just to make the guys look like angry husbands.

* * *

I couldn't remember ever seeing the newspaper article about my
father's arrest and assumed I found out about it the same way I
found out about everything in Tulsa: from my mother. Years later,
I wanted to see the article for myself, so I called the Tulsa County
Library and asked to speak with a research librarian. For a small
fee, the research department would be happy to search two weeks
of newspapers, but they could not look through months and
months. I thought it had happened in the fall of 1972 but had
nothing more exact than that.

I tried searching online and looking though my old journals,
but I turned up no clues. Finally, I called my mother and asked
her. Though long divorced from my father by 1972, Mother
remembered quite a lot about the arrest.

Mother said it happened the spring that she, Vol, and Bonnie went
to Hawaii. They had asked me to go along, but as she recalled, I
chose to go somewhere else instead. When they got back from their
trip, Vol was working out in the yard when a neighbor came over
to chat and happened to mention that a Tulsa doctor named Stokes
had been arrested for doing illegal abortions. The neighbor didn't
seem to know that my mother had been married to that Dr. Stokes.

Mother said she didn't tell me about the arrest. A former boyfriend
from Tulsa, who was a student at Amherst, was home over spring
break and learned of the arrest. When he went back to Amherst, as
Mother said, he started spreading the information around. He must
have told my former roommate, Phyllis, who was an exchange
student at Amherst that year, and she told me. I have no memory of
getting the news, but that version of the story makes sense.

Mother went on to say, "He spent the night in jail."

When I commented that I had always assumed it was true, she said,
"Malcolm did abortions. Judy [a family friend] told me that when
she went out to T.U. [Tulsa University] and pledged a sorority, the
girls told her that if she got into trouble, to call Dr. Stokes." This

must have taken Judy by surprise, since Mother reported that Judy exclaimed, "He delivered me!"

Mother went on to say that there was another doctor in town who did abortions, though she couldn't remember his name. She thought he had moved to Tulsa during the Depression, had a hard time making a living, and so started doing abortions. "If the woman got into trouble, bleeding or something, [that doctor] would send her to Malcolm."

Mother said my father was arrested somewhere up around the lake where he lived but not at his house. He had gone to another place. She also recalled that a woman had been taken somewhere in an ambulance.

After sifting through a box of old letters, I came across a postcard from Vol, dated March 30, 1972, written from Hawaii, saying that they had been to see a volcano and wishing me a good trip to Florida.

Of course! I was in Florida. I spent spring vacation of my junior year in Florida with Sally Patton and her *a cappella* singing group, the Whims. The group gave several concerts, we toured Disney World, which was brand new, and I had one dinner with Bob, an Amherst student I had a crush on.

With Vol's postcard in hand, I called the Tulsa library and asked a researcher to look for the story of my father's arrest in the paper just before and after March 30, 1972. That afternoon, I received an e-mail with the front-page story attached.

Tulsa World
Sunday March 26, 1972

Headline: *Tulsa Doctor Arrested In Lake Abortion Raid*

An unidentified woman, who police said had apparently undergone an abortion, was in a Tulsa Hospital Saturday after being found in a Lake Keystone house late Friday when law enforcement officials arrested three Tulsans, including an obstetrician.

Dr. Elmer Malcolm Stokes, 54, Charles Getter, 46, and David Stuart Taylor were arrested when law enforcement officials, armed with a search warrant, raided the house late Friday.

The three were released on bonds Saturday and are to appear in Pawnee County District Court at 10 a.m. Tuesday. Stokes and Fetter were freed on $3,000 bonds each, and Taylor was released on $5,000 bond.

No charges have been filed. Pawnee County Dist. Atty. Bill Hall said, "They won't be filed until Monday because the courthouse is closed."

Legal action is centered in Pawnee County, where the house is located.

Officials connected with the case refused Saturday to give further information on the woman. All police would say is that she apparently had just "undergone an abortion."

Police said the basement of the unfinished house resembled "a medical facility," with what appeared to be an operating room and eight patient rooms, each with a couch and television set.

A quantity of medical equipment police described as "quite complete" was confiscated.

The raid by nine law enforcement officials from Pawnee and Tulsa counties capped a week-long investigation, police said.

Pawnee County Dist. Judge O. S. Palmer issued a search warrant Friday after officials alleged there was "probable cause" to indicate the house was being used for abortions.

Tulsa police who participated in the raid said their assistance had been requested by Pawnee County officials.

At the time of his arrest, Fetter was free on bond on an abortion conspiracy charge filed in connection with a police raid in November 1970 at what police termed an "abortion mill" in Tulsa.

Taylor had been convicted in 1968 of burglary of an airplane at Riverside Airport, police records showed.

Fetter and Taylor gave their address as an apartment house at 3238 S. Yale Ave.

Stokes, a 1961 appointee to the state Mental Health Board, earlier this week told police he lives at 4323 S. Riverside Drive.

The address was given when Stokes told police he was missing luggage used in a plane trip which contained $8,785 in jewelry.

Police would not comment on events leading to the raid.

Hall said he didn't think there was any connection between the raid and a statement made by a Tulsa psychologist during a state Legislature hearing on an abortion bill this year.

The psychologist claimed that an abortionist was operating out of the east side of Tulsa "and it's a poor weekend when he doesn't make $2,000."

Police said they believed the Lake Keystone house had been used as an abortion clinic for "several months."

Tulsa attorney Roehm West who with Irvine Underman is defending the trio said Stokes was a "complete victim of circumstances." He said Stokes had sold his boat to Fetter and "was going to pick up payment on the boat."

"Fetter had called him Friday and told him he had bleeding ulcers and wanted him to bring him some medicine and pick up payment on the boat."

"Doc was backing his car out of the driveway when the constabulary came. They ordered him back inside," West said.

West also is the attorney for W. J. Bryan Henrie, a former Gove osteopath, in a suit challenging the constitutionality of Oklahoma's abortion laws. Henrie served a prison term after admitting he was an abortionist.

In addition to the medical equipment, officials confiscated a gun during the raid. Officers said the weapon was taken from Taylor.

The house is located in the Ridgemont Estates Addition, 6.7 miles west of Lake Keystone dam on U.S. 64.

Contractor Gene Ames said the house had been under construction periodically for 19 months.

My father was arraigned but never tried. It was late 1972, and everyone knew that the Supreme Court was about to deliberate on Roe v. Wade. By January 22, 1973, my father's alleged activities were no longer illegal. At least I wouldn't have to discuss a trial with my friends and relatives. I was relieved but still embarrassed.

Actually, I was mortified. I had survived my parents' divorce, was doing nicely in college, and was about to be launched into the world and then this! My father was caught doing something that, if not illegal, was certainly frowned on in Oklahoma. I tried not to think about it.

My mother, who had watched my father get himself out of a succession of binds over the years, mostly financial in nature, remarked that, "This time the Supreme Court bailed him out." If my father's life hadn't turned out sadly in the end, I'd say he was a golden boy and that things always worked out for him. He had an enormous capacity to make events happen the way he wanted. He had great initiative; he just wasn't very good at maintenance. His gold tarnished over time. His relationships faltered, his health deteriorated, and the admiration of his oldest daughter collapsed.

While living in Greensboro, North Carolina, in the late 1970s, I served on the board of NARAL-NC, the state chapter of the National Abortion Rights Action League. Many of the people on the board were doctors, clinic owners, or women who had had abortions. After being elected as the president of the board, I realized I was there because of my dad. His pioneering work, providing safe abortions before they were legal, was a motivation for me to work to keep abortions safe and legal. Daddy was dead by then, so I couldn't talk with him about it, but somewhere in my ever-expanding feminist consciousness, I had turned my shame into a modicum of pride and into action.

Twenty-One
Conversion
1972

In the autumn of 1972, I was a senior in college and was falling in love with Ed, a tall, gangly slow-spoken man from North Carolina. Though a student at Smith College, I was living nine miles down the road at Amherst College as an "exchange student" for the year. Living at a men's college precipitated the only dramatic conversion experience of my life—a conversion to feminism.

That fall was as crisp and breathtakingly beautiful as the three previous ones I had spent in New England, and I thought it was a real boon to be one of the only women students living on an otherwise all-male campus. Well, all male except for the scores of women who stayed over with their boyfriends and the twenty-four of us who were in residence for the year.

One afternoon, I was walking across the quad in front of Robert Frost Library, kicking up fall leaves as I went, and thinking how lucky I was to have all these men to myself, when I stopped dead in my tracks. Suddenly struck by the error of my ways, I reconsidered what I had just been thinking. All these men, twelve hundred of them, who ate breakfast like barnyard animals, who made jokes about women as they walked by, who thought they were smarter and better than anyone else—these were the people I thought were a special gift to me? I stood stone-still and asked myself, *Who had been my best support all my life? Guys, my Dad, boyfriends?* My father had all but disappeared. When I broke up with boyfriends, they vanished from my life. It was women who remained—my mother, Sally, other childhood girlfriends, my friends at Smith. Who did I imagine would stay with me and support me in the future? The women! It was as though I took my head in my hands in that moment and turned it in the direction of women. "I'm going to pay attention to women," I promised. "I'm going to listen to them, and stop over-valuing men. I'm going to stop looking for everything from men, who can't or won't give it to me." I still liked men, I was just clear that I'd stop acting like they were the only important people on the planet.

* * *

After graduation, I followed Ed to North Carolina, where I spent a year working at odd jobs and applying to graduate schools, including seminaries. In the spring of 1974, Duke Divinity School hosted the second Inter-Seminary Women's Conference, and I attended. A few Duke women had attended the first such conference, held at Yale the year before, and offered to host the second one. When I entered Duke as a divinity student in the fall of 1974, the Duke Divinity Women's Center was just opening its doors. It was the first women's center on the campus, pre-dating the university's women's center and the Women's Studies program. When the first Divinity Women's Center director left in May to take a summer placement out of state, I stepped in for three months. When she decided to remain out of state, I became the second director.

In my seminary classes, I tended to ask the same question over and over, "What about the women?" Sometimes I got blank stares from professors and sometimes suggestions for ways to begin my own research. While I worked in the Women's Center, I helped set up women's studies classes on such topics as "women in ministry" and "women and pastoral counseling."

Near the end of my third year, I went to see my beloved mentor, Helen Crotwell, the Associate Minister to the University, to discuss my future. I had no idea what I was going to do. When I suggested I might just look for a job in a local church, she said I had never indicated that I wanted to be a parish minister and suggested I do something that no one else was going to do, though she didn't know what that might be.

After graduation in 1977, I traveled to see friends who were serving churches in the South and discovered that they wanted someone to care they existed and to get them together. I started the Resource Center for Women and Ministry in the South (RCWMS) that fall and persuaded Helen Crotwell to be one of the original trustees. Later that fall, I moved to Greensboro, the town where my college boyfriend was living. Even though I had broken up with Ed the year before, I think I was still in love with him.

Once in Greensboro, I continued to develop RCWMS, worked for the passage of the Equal Rights Amendment, organized Susan B. Anthony birthday parties, and agreed to chair the state board of the National Abortion Rights Action League in North Carolina (NARAL-NC). As I look back on those years, I see so many connections with my uncle and my father. I was working on social justice issues from a faith perspective, as my uncle had, and on women's health issues that were near to my father's heart. In my twenties, however, I was still so mad at my father that I ignored the ways I had been influenced by the Stokes clan.

While in Greensboro, I fell in love with Katherine, a reporter at the city newspaper. Soon after our partnership began, she took on the challenge of being the first editor of *The Independent*, a progressive newspaper based in Durham, and started commuting fifty miles to work. After five years of Katherine's wearing herself out driving back and forth, I gave in and moved back to Durham, taking RCWMS along.

Then, in early 1990, I fell in love with John and moved to Philadelphia, a city with way too much concrete. We lived downtown, where I could see only one tree from our apartment window. I kept saying, "Just get me back over the state line into North Carolina." We got married that fall, John finished his work in Philadelphia, and we moved back to Durham. We bought the wonderful house in which I still live, tried to get pregnant (unsuccessfully), and got a divorce. All that took about eight years, but that's the gist of it.

I think I confused John with my father, just as I had my college boyfriend. John was short, cute, smart, athletic, willing to work, and had scrambled up from humble beginnings, like my father. Plus he was a vegetarian and from Texas; how could I resist? He had my father's charisma, but not his warmth, and while there was plenty of drama in the marriage, there wasn't a lot of emotional connection. I wrote a whole book about getting over that marriage, *Hurricane Season*.

What the separation and divorce did for me is the interesting part: it cracked me open like a walnut. The day John called to say the marriage was over, I vowed *not* to be a good sport, *not* to say I was fine, but to weep and wail, and to say just how horrible it was to be left. As I grieved the loss of my marriage, it felt as though I was also grieving the loss of my father years before. In the process, I stopped being so afraid of my feelings. I learned that if waves of sadness began to wash over me, I could lie down and let them. I didn't have to control them. I learned that no one gets through unscathed, that life is designed to break our hearts, and that what really counts is what we make out of what happens to us. Everything can be like compost in a bin. With time and a little attention, a stinky pile of bad experiences can turn into the fertile soil of life.

The marriage broke up in 1997. Over the next few years, as I lived through the hurt, the anger, and the healing, a new openness to my father began to develop. Something shifted in me, and I began to be more and more curious about him. By then, Uncle Henry had died and Aunt Mary Beth was slowly fading away. As my cousins sorted through their parents' papers, they kept finding things they thought I might like to have. In 2000, when Beth sent me the letters Daddy wrote to Henry in the early 1940s, my father appeared before me as a young man, a version of him I had never met before. When Sharon called five years later to say Jere was dying, I was ready to make a trip to Georgia, to be with his people and in his native land.

Twenty-Two
Fear of Flying
1970s

By the time I graduated from college and moved to North
Carolina, I had pretty much given up flying. The breakdown of
my relationship with airplanes started during Thanksgiving break
of my senior year. Mother, Vol, Bonnie, and I were sitting around
the dining room table when Vol said, "I've always wanted to see
Mt. Everest." Before the meal was over, the four of us had decided
we should go to Nepal. Vol's business had been doing well, and
it seemed like a good time for a big trip. While I was back in
school, Vol selected countries with mountain ranges (Morocco
for the Atlas, Iran for the Alborz, Nepal for the Himalayas), and
Mother arranged stops in between (Casablanca, Rome, New Delhi,
Bangkok, Hong Kong, Tokyo, and Honolulu.)

We left the U.S. on December 21, 1972 and had Christmas in
Morocco, with palm trees. We stayed in fine hotels, had airplanes
nearly to ourselves, and had only a few travel glitches. We were
delayed by a blizzard in Tehran, we each got sick at least once, and
there was some confusion about our hotel reservations when we
arrived in Kathmandu, but that got sorted out.

The weather in the mountains was bad while we were in Nepal,
so we never got to see Mt. Everest up close. As a consolation,
Vol arranged for a helicopter pilot to take us to a high mountain
village. I snapped pictures of Tibetan prayer flags in front of a
Buddhist temple in the tiny enclave. A small round-faced girl with
an even smaller child tied to her back caught my attention in the
Himalayan village, and I captured them on film. I took pictures
everywhere we went on that trip, just as I had in Hawaii and Japan
when I was ten, but of all the pictures from various trips, the one

of those children's faces remains a favorite. Inside one of the village huts, I remarked on the dark ceiling and asked how it got to be so black. I was imagining many coats of lacquer. "Soot from the fire," the pilot explained as I noticed the house had no chimney or smoke hole.

We flew from Kathmandu to Pokhara in an old DC-3. Popular with tourists for its exquisite view, Pokhara faces the 26,545-foot summit of Annapurna, the "Fish Tail" mountain with its pointy concave peak. On the way, our plane landed at Tiger Tops, a game preserve, to take on passengers. While standing around on the grass airstrip, the pilot glanced at the plane and said, "This thing doesn't always crank when I turn the key." My breath caught. We were halfway around the world, and I had managed to experience most of the flying as a great adventure. The plane started up just fine, but ever since, I have been afraid that I used up all my flying luck on that airplane. I didn't develop a fear of flying right away, but the seed was planted.

The DC-3 was a much more reliable plane than I knew. Decades later, I fell into a conversation with a man who had lived in Nepal around the time I was there. His comment on the DC-3 was, "Best airplane ever made." The aircraft was known for flying "over the Hump" during World War II, an important supply route over the Himalayas that was used after the Japanese closed the Burma Road and shut off the route from Thailand to China.

Not knowing anything of that, the pilot's comment only frightened me. I didn't understand that he probably meant that if the plane started, it would certainly fly.

Sometime after the trip to Nepal, I stopped wanting to fly. I didn't panic on airplanes, but by the mid-1970s I simply refused to get on them. I had flown all my life and all over the world, on commercial planes, in my father's Cessna 180, on prop planes and jets, in a helicopter over the Himalayas, in a DC-3 turned passenger carrier, over the Atlantic and the Pacific and the Mekong Delta, to Hawaii, Europe, and the Caribbean. I was twenty-four or twenty-five.

I was living in North Carolina by then and felt at home. It was as though I simply folded my wings and was done. I wanted to stay on the ground and remember persuading my boyfriend Ed to drive to Oklahoma with me at least once. Mother said my refusing to fly was a mechanism of control, words I'm sure she learned from the same reliable shrink who taught her to say *shit* and to stand up to my stepfather. She may have been right. If I didn't want to go to Oklahoma for Christmas, or Thanksgiving, or my birthday any more, I could develop a fear of flying and quit.

I've never entirely understood my fear of flying. It wasn't a typical "panic on the airplane" kind of fear. Once I get on a plane, I'm fine (well, fine enough). I simply resign myself to the fact that the plane might blow up at any moment or cut off and fall out of the sky. (Detailed explanations from aeronautical engineers didn't help. Never mind about the theory; machines fail!)

A decade later, in the late 1980s, Katherine got me to agree to go to England with her, but only because she agreed to go on a boat. I felt certain I would get on that plane to come home. Since then, I have mostly only been willing to fly for things I'm willing to die for, things like seeing Sally, my mother, Tuscany, or Paris. For comfort on the plane, I tell myself that I'll either get to meet Jesus or arrive at my destination.

As a child I thought I was safe in my family, safe standing on the front seat beside my mother or grandmother while they drove the car, safe flying in my father's airplane. Then my parents' marriage disintegrated, the federal government announced it was not safe for children to stand up in the front seat, and I learned that pilots and doctors had some of the highest rates of alcoholism in the country. So not only did I need to worry about the plane exploding, I had to worry about the guy in the cockpit as well. (In the 1970s, most of them were guys.)

Once I noticed the dangers of flying, I worried. But then I'm the person who used to worry that the front wheel of my bicycle might fall off. (I don't think it is even physically possible.)

I'll stop talking about scary things, except to say that when I reach for the phone, or now the computer, to make a plane reservation, death and destruction always come to mind. I'm grateful to have gone so many interesting places back in the *good old days* when flying was still fun.

Twenty-Three
Longing for Lowcountry
2008

In January 2008, I became obsessed with the photograph I have of Maggie Seabrook, the woman who worked for my father's family when he was young. I wanted to know who she was and had enough practice tracking down my own ancestors that I decided to try my hand at finding Maggie Seabrook's. I wondered if I could find out anything about who she was or where she had come from.

The picture was dated 1944. The closest census data available to the public was 1930, so I looked at that year's census records for Maggie Seabrook in Savannah, Georgia. Bingo! There was one. She was fifty-five years old, living with her eighty-seven-year-old father, William E. Seabrook. Her occupation was listed as "servant" in a private family.

I tried the census for 1920, and there she was again, a lodger living with a black couple and working as a chambermaid in a boarding house. Perhaps my great-grandmother's boarding house on Jones Street, though my great-grandmother was dead by then.

I looked further back and found a William Seabrook in 1870, twenty-seven years old (the right age to be the same man as Maggie's father), born in South Carolina, working as a painter, and living in Beaufort, SC. Then I noticed two columns of the record that indicated he could read and write. What? That was the South Carolina Lowcountry, five years after the end of the Civil War, and an African American man named William Seabrook can read. It seemed odd to me.

I looked up Beaufort, South Carolina, on the Internet and found that the Union controlled Beaufort and the surrounding area for most of the War and that the Penn School had been set up on St. Helena Island in 1862 to educate former slaves. I wanted to know more about Beaufort and the islands nearby.

Help was on the way, though I didn't recognize it at first. An Episcopal priest in Chapel Hill named Liz e-mailed saying she wanted to have lunch and talk about writing. That was February and I was busy. Then Liz got the flu. Then I went to Spain and France for two weeks in the spring. Four months later, we managed to make a date for lunch at a bakery in Durham. All I knew about Liz was that she was a priest, a writer, had blonde hair, and would be wearing a blue dress with fish on it.

In the first few minutes of our conversation, I learned that Liz was my age, had grown up in Beaufort, South Carolina, which she reminded me was pronounced BU-fert (as in *beautiful*), unlike the town on the coast in North Carolina which is pronounced BOW-fort. She was a student at Radcliffe when I was at Smith, and she graduated from Duke Divinity School. The coincidences were so startling that I almost choked on my fish tacos. I told her I was working on a book about my father, had been reading about Georgia, and was interested in Maggie Seabrook. I said it was sad that in the 1920s the daughter of a literate man had to work as a nursemaid, to which Liz replied, "And that was a *good* job."

When I told Liz that Maggie Seabrook had led me to Beaufort and the Penn School, she told me the Civil War history of the area. In 1861, the Union Navy went up the Beaufort River and took control of the area. The white citizens of Beaufort did not fight but fled, leaving behind their houses in town, plantations on nearby St. Helena Island, and thousands of enslaved African Americans who had been growing cotton and rice. Union officers occupied houses in town, and furnishings in the unoccupied houses were carried off. After the war the black people got some of the land, and the struggle to hang onto it began.

Liz said her family still owned a cottage on St. Helena and that we should go there sometime. She suggested I read *The Port Royal Experiment* (pronounced "Pot Ral") for a general history of the area and Laura Towne's diary to learn more about the Penn School. Laura Towne went south as a missionary in the early 1860s and started the school, which she ran with her friend, Ellen Murray, for forty years. It was the first educational experiment of Reconstruction. Evidently some Northerners were not sure former slaves could learn to read.

That afternoon after lunch with Liz, I went back to my office and looked the books up on the Internet. Duke had a copy of *The Port Royal Experiment*, so I called my former intern Candice on her cell phone and reached her at the bus stop near the Duke library. I proposed that if she would check out the book for me, I'd come pick her up and drive her home. Half an hour later, I had the book in hand.

As for Laura Towne's diary, I discovered that the University of North Carolina in Chapel Hill owned the original diary as well as a very old copy that was still in circulation. I asked a friend who was doing research in the UNC library to check it out for me, and I had it a couple of days later.

I was fascinated by the Gullah language, which black people on the Sea Islands near Charleston and Savannah once spoke. Liz mentioned that the woman who took care of her when she was small was a Gullah speaker. When Liz went to the first grade, no one could understand her.

I had read an essay by Duke professor Tim Tyson on the development of languages among immigrants, a process he called creolization. When people come to a place with a language different from their own, new immigrants often create a language by mixing the new language with their own, in order to communicate. The amalgamation is called a pidgin language. Over time, as the hybrid language is used, the patterns of speech and vocabulary stabilize, people teach it to their children, and it becomes what is known as *creole*. Languages, cultures, the landscape had merged to form the Lowcountry where my father grew up, and for months I had been wanting to see it, hear it, smell it again.

When my friend Sally called a few weeks later and said she wanted to go to Savannah in August, I jumped at the chance. I could follow my obsession about Maggie Seabrook and visit my oldest cousin Gail, who lived in Beaufort. She had known my father before I was born and was quite fond of him. I wanted to ask her questions about my father and about our grandparents. I was going to the Lowcountry again, in August, the hottest month of the year.

Twenty-Four
Drifting South
2008

Sally and I grew up in Tulsa, where summer was long and hot; but Sally spent much of her adult life in Boston, where summers were never warm enough to suit her. She wanted to go to Savannah because it promised warmth and charm. I had wanted to return to Savannah ever since my quick trip there in 2005. We agreed to spend a couple of nights with Gail in Beaufort and a couple in Savannah.

Sally flew to North Carolina as planned and spent a few days in Durham. We try to see one another at least once a year, and this visit gave her a chance to spend some time with Dwight, my new husband of two years. Sally's birthday was that weekend, so she and I celebrated by gathering a few female friends and attending an outdoor concert at the North Carolina Museum of Art. We packed salads, hummus, and Sally's favorite pimento cheese spread into a cooler and arrived early enough to enjoy our picnic before the music began. Our conversation wandered into politics. It was clear that Barack Obama would be the Democratic candidate for president, but many of us were nervous about whether an African American man could get elected in our racist country. As the evening light faded and the stars came out, the friendly crowd and rockabilly music made me feel hopeful in every way.

The outdoor concert was a good way to begin the journey south to my father's homeland. Sitting outside on a warm summer night, chatting with friends and listening to live music would have delighted my dad. He'd have been drinking, laughing, and holding a cigar in his teeth while clapping his approval of the musicians. He loved live performances. The year we lived in New York, he was constantly taking my mother into the city to Broadway musicals or to clubs to hear cabaret singers. I began to sense my father's presence drifting nearby like smoke from one of his cigars.

My father's influence continued the next morning. While getting ready to leave on the trip with Sally, I was running behind schedule if we were going to get to Gail's by 4:00 p.m. as promised. I figured I was just getting in sync with my father, who was notoriously late. (He used to ask my mother to call the airport and ask them to hold a plane. "Tell 'em the doctor's delivering a baby," he'd say when he was simply late. Sometimes the airport would actually oblige.)

Our drive to Beaufort was long but uneventful. I drove some and Sally drove some. We stopped at a rest area in South Carolina to eat the lunch I had packed, but it was so hard to eat with one hand and shoo flies with the other that we gobbled our salads, packed up, and jumped back in the car. The gnats that followed us into the car reminded me that we were indeed headed farther south, where summer is all about bugs.

As we got closer to the Lowcountry, I began to yearn for it. I wanted to smell the marshy ground, to drive around St. Helena Island and see the Penn Center, now an African American educational and cultural center. I wasn't sure what else. My heart was longing for something, but for what?

When we got off the interstate and onto Highway 17, the coastal highway, the signs along the road read *Lowcountry* this and *Lowcountry* that. Ditches flanked the eight-mile road from the highway to Beaufort, low fields stood flooded with water, and Spanish moss hung off the trees. I saw a sign on the right, "Seabrook, 1 Mile." Seabrook, like Maggie Seabrook! Had her people actually lived here? We didn't have time to stop, but I was so excited that I wanted to plan my next trip to Beaufort before we even reached the town.

As the road meandered past inlets and through wetlands, I felt as though I had slipped into the opening sequence of the movie *Prince of Tides*. Shot from a plane flying low over the marshes of the southern coast, that sequence contains some of my favorite images in the world. When Sally had asked, before the trip, if we would be able to see water, I had assured her that there would be water everywhere. And indeed there was. The landscape is much like broken dinner plates scattered on the floor. The pieces represent the land, and all the space in between is water.

* * *

We reached Beaufort by 4:00 p.m., in plenty of time for the 5:00 church service.

When Gail and Bill had retired to Beaufort a decade before, they looked forward to joining the local Episcopal church, the historic St. Helena's. Established in 1712, the stately building was constructed of English bricks once used as ship's ballast. Though the edifice was appealing, they soon discovered that St. Helena's was one of the most conservative churches in one of the most conservative dioceses in the country. The next Episcopal church was over half an hour away.

Gail was distraught to have landed in what felt like nineteenth-century Christendom. Her father left the Baptists over their conservative stance on race, and she had become an Episcopalian as he had. Bill was a retired United Methodist clergyman and a progressive one at that. They simply weren't interested in being part of a congregation where they'd be so out of step. Eventually they found like-minded Episcopalians in town and started meeting as a small group on Sunday evenings, first as a Bible study, then for Eucharist led by a retired priest, and finally for full-blown worship services with Gail, a life-long piano teacher, on the electric piano. They called themselves St. Mark's Chapel.

Gail's daughter Melissa was visiting from Kansas City, so the five of us went to set up for the 5:00 p.m. service, which was held at a small motel downtown. I spent a good part of the actual service fumbling with the prayer book, but it ended soon enough, and I enjoyed meeting the people in my cousin's new community of faith.

After church, Bill drove us around Beaufort's historic district. Two- and three-story buildings with fine porches lined the shady streets. We piled out of the car to stare through the fence at the grand house used in *The Big Chill*, a story of another nostalgic reunion, and I expected to see Kevin Kline come bounding down the front stairs with boxes of running shoes in his arms. We finished our outing with dinner at a great Thai restaurant, and I considered it a perfect first date with a new town.

***

Sally and I stayed near Gail and Bill in the house of neighbors who were out of town. On Monday, I took a morning walk around the neighborhood before Sally and I had breakfast on the screened porch of our borrowed house. As I ate the yogurt and peaches I had brought from home, I told myself the sticky breathless morning was not so bad, considering it was August in the Lowcountry. I managed to sit outside long enough to write a few lines in my journal.

That morning on my walk, I had noticed a black woman standing in the doorway of a house I passed. "Puppy, do you want to come inside?" she asked a dog in the yard. At first I thought she was the help, but caught myself. Couldn't there be black people living in the neighborhood? Either way, whether it was her dog or her employer's dog, she was being very polite. When the small fluffy dog trotted toward me, I tried to deter it with, "Go home, puppy." She said, "I was just asking him if he wanted to come inside." "I'll try to look disinterested," I responded. She smiled and laughed amiably as I turned to walk on down the street.

A world of history had passed between the two of us, and I was full of questions. Did she own the house? Was she a local? She was very well-spoken and didn't seem to have a local accent. Was she friendly because people in Beaufort are nice, because she was polite, or because my people terrorized her grandparents and she was taught that being nice might save her life? Was Maggie Seabrook that polite when a stranger spoke to her as she rocked a white baby on my grandmother's porch? I wondered how she might have influenced my father. Had she tried to teach him to be warm and friendly to override his mother's cold suspicious nature? Had she shaped his relationship to black people? I had no idea and no memories or stories to go on.

I had just completed *The South in Black and White*, a course on the history of race in the South taught by historian Tim Tyson, author of *Blood Done Sign My Name*. The class was a reminder that the evils of slavery did not end with the Civil War, that the period of Reconstruction was a nightmare for black people, and that by the 1960s, black people had nothing that approached equal treatment or equal rights.

I remembered the outdoor concert two nights before. Sitting next to a dark-skinned woman, I had noticed how aware I am of color. I sort by color, almost unconsciously, whether I mean to or not. I must have been taught to do it. And though I no longer ascribe value along with skin color, I still notice. *That person is darker than that one. This one is lighter than that one.* The truth is that we are all mixed up together. We are all related in the South, and for generations we had all been taught to sort by color.

I had asked my mother about her family's attitudes about race. Her mother's mother was born into a family that owned slaves. My grandmother was less prejudiced than her mother, but only a little. My mother less so than her mother, but she still freaked out one time when she thought the curly-headed man I said I was dating might be black. He was Italian.

I remember almost nothing of my father's attitudes toward African Americans. When I was very small, we had a black housekeeper named Dorothy, whom I adored, but she and my father don't appear together in any of my memories. Tulsa was segregated in the 1950s, and he moved in a white world. Though my father grew up in a city that was roughly fifty percent African American, and was cared for by a black woman when he was small, I was drawing a blank on his attitudes about race.

Sitting on the porch in Beaufort, South Carolina, staring out on a small patch of woods, I imagined the souls of slave holders and of enslaved people wandering the sandy roads of Beaufort County and St. Helena Island in search of understanding, just as I had been wandering about trying to understand my father and the land of his birth.

Twenty-Five
St. Helena Island
2008

Before I left my perch on the back porch, I closed my eyes and drank in the raspy chorus of cicadas in the trees just beyond the yard. To me it was the sound of summer in the South. My father grew up with that sound in his ears. He must have fallen asleep on summer nights, windows open and sheets sticking to his moist skin, with that squeaky chorus singing his lullaby.

I gathered everything I might need for the day: camera, sunscreen, walking shoes, journal, sweater, phone, computer, bathing suit, and a towel. Sally and I picked up Melissa and drove into Beaufort's small but charming downtown to poke around in shops and find a place for lunch. In the bookstore on Bay Street, I bought a copy of the Bible translated into Gullah, one book by the former director of the Penn Center, a short history of Port Royal, and two boxes of Jonathan Green cards. Green's brightly colored Lowcountry paintings pleased me as much as anything. When I see them now, I can almost smell the mud of the Lowcountry.

It was a bright blue day and I was happy to be in Beaufort, though I still felt slightly unsettled. I wanted to get on out to St. Helena without rushing my time with Melissa. I wanted to get on with my search, though I didn't really know what I was hunting for and could only hope that I'd know it when I came across it. I had picked up the wrong camera while packing for the trip, one that required film, and I didn't have any film. I was afraid that if I found what I was looking for, I wouldn't be able to take a picture of it. After lunch and a time of resting on the waterfront, Sally and I returned Melissa to Gail's house, stopped at a drugstore so I could buy film, and set off for St. Helena Island. ·

The islands around Beaufort are separated by so many creeks and inlets that you are always driving over bridges to get anywhere. We crossed the bridge to Lady's Island and followed the two-lane road through areas of maritime forest and areas of cultivated fields. In another ten minutes, we crossed onto St. Helena and were pulling into the parking area at the Penn Center. Low white buildings rested comfortably under the shade of giant live oak trees. Minimal signage left me wondering where to begin.

As I headed toward the door of the closest building, I could feel myself moving into the overly solicitous part of my personality. That's the white liberal overcompensating part that tries to treat African Americans like royalty to offset how badly my ancestors treated theirs and to ward off any residual anger on their part. If I'm really nice, maybe they won't be mad with me for the whole 250-year history of slavery in America. *Good plan, Jeanette.* I do it almost unconsciously, except that I always feel a slightly uncomfortable shift inside.

Once inside, I asked politely where I might find the museum I had read about. It was in the building next door. *Good, no one has yelled, "White girl, go home," at me yet.* The museum, originally built as a schoolhouse, had a wide central hall and evenly balanced wings on either side. Inside, an elderly black man in a dark blue tee-shirt and denim shorts greeted me and explained that he was a volunteer and was available to give tours of the island after the museum closed at 4:00 p.m. I said I might want a tour, thinking he might be able to explain the Lowcountry to me.

Sally and I wandered through the exhibits in the small museum. I breezed through, pausing at photographs of women in long dresses of the period I had been reading about in Laura Towne's diary, but was more interested in getting out and seeing the island than poring over the history of the school's curriculum. While standing in front of the last wall of photographs, I noticed a handsome African American man walk into the exhibit area. He looked familiar. I glanced again at the warm broad face and finally walked right up to him, "Cal?" "Jeanette?" he responded. "What are you doing here?" I asked. He had come for a meeting, and before I could explain that I was in Beaufort visiting a cousin, a woman from my women's group in Durham came around the corner. "Cynthia!" I exclaimed, and we both started laughing. "Girl, what brings you here?" she asked, and I explained I was trying to get to know the particular area in which my father grew up. When I realized Cynthia and Cal were part of the same event, I inquired about another friend who often worked with them, "Is Alan with you?" "Yes." Oh, this was all too funny. There I was at the end of the road, and I bumped into people I knew. "See, this always happens," Sally piped in. "It doesn't matter where we go, Jeanette always runs into people she knows." Did I need to come all that way to be reminded I am my father's daughter?

I got involved in talking with my friends, meeting the director of the Penn Center, buying a reprint of *Laura Towne's Diary*, and trying to talk Cal into a copy of *God, Dr. Buzzard and the Bolito Man*, a wonderful book about the Sea Islands. Meanwhile, Sally was ready to go. She had determined that the tour would cost us twenty dollars apiece and would cover the whole island. "Come on Jeanette," she said, "our guide is waiting."

I snapped a picture of my North Carolina friends, and then Sally and I got in a big red truck with the man who had greeted me at the front door for our tour of the island Laura Towne had described.

* * *

Robert Middleton climbed nimbly into the driver's seat of his big red truck. Sally got in front and I took the backseat where I could write more comfortably. The seventy-nine-year-old dark-skinned man who pronounced his name "Milton" was raised on St. Helena and attended the Penn School but had to quit in the eleventh grade to help out on the farm. Pulling out of the parking area, Mr. Middleton explained that although there were no longer plantations on the island, many areas still carried their names.

My favorite of all the names is Frogmore. Our guide explained an early owner had named that section for his ancestral home in England. The peculiar name is preserved in a traditional

Lowcountry seafood boil, Frogmore stew. I imagined enormous cast-iron pots of shrimp, sausages, corn, and potatoes simmering over open fires.

As we bounced along the narrow ribbon of asphalt that allows modern vehicles to move about on the island, Mr. Middleton talked and I scribbled as fast as I could, as though attending an important college lecture. I didn't want to miss anything. Martin Luther King, Jr., came to St. Helena when he was working on his speech for Washington, DC, our guide announced. The island was a favorite retreat for the civil rights leader. At the time of his assassination, he was in the process of building a house at the Penn Center.

Land on the island was originally worked by slaves, many from rice-growing regions of West Africa. Captured Africans were brought to the Sea Islands to grow rice, indigo, cotton, and spices, working alongside Native American laborers and European indentured servants. The mix of cultures and the geographical isolation produced a unique culture, known as Gullah.

"After the war, all the land went to black families," Mr. Middleton said. I knew he meant the Civil War. "Still, a lot is owned by black families," he added. Land retention has long been an issue for the African American people of St. Helena, as in the rest of the South. Northerners gave black people land during Reconstruction but sometimes failed to convey the proper deeds. Some people lost their land for taxes they didn't know they owed. Others lost it to unscrupulous land traders. Today, developers are the biggest danger.

When Mr. Middleton was a boy, most of the fifteen-mile-long, eight-mile-wide island was farmed, with rice growing in the lowlands and sugar cane and cotton on higher ground. (I realized Mr. Middleton was describing rural life in the Lowcountry when my father was growing up in nearby Savannah, so I paid close attention.) He said the people caught fish, shrimp, and crab. His father worked for himself, farming, fishing, and making wooden boats to sell. Mr. Middleton didn't like making nets; he said it was too hard. Everybody on the island used to work Monday to Saturday noon doing farm work. They cooked on Saturday afternoon and went to church on Sunday.

Since the island was large and churches were far apart, small prayer houses sprang up in neighborhoods, so people could gather several nights of the week to pray and sing the old songs. We stopped and went in one tiny house of worship that was smaller than a two-car garage.

The island people used to grow or make nearly everything they needed and shared with nearby folks in need. Farming had declined in recent years, and trees had filled in. Now, Hispanics do what farm work there is left. Black folks have other jobs like carpentry or bricklaying. Mr. Middleton lamented that it had been hard to keep young people on St. Helena, though it was a little easier now that there was a training school on the island.

I admired the Spanish moss dripping from the leafy canopy shading the roadway and wondered whether the moss hurt the trees. "You can't touch those trees," Mr. Middleton said, explaining that regulations protected the live oak trees from being cut down.

On Seaside Road, with cultivated land to our left and water to the right, he mentioned that the black cemeteries on the island were near the water, because people believed that the tides would take their spirits home to Africa. I wondered about my father's grave in Oklahoma and wondered whether his spirit was trying to get back to the sea.

* * *

After the tour, Sally and I stopped at the Brick Baptist Church to locate the graves of Laura Towne and Ellen Murray. The tall stone markers stood side-by-side, just as they had for nearly a hundred years. Laura and Ellen lived and worked side by side for forty years, and I was glad the local people saw fit to bury them next to each other. I thought of them as heroines, missionaries, early women in ministry. Their courage, imagination, and willingness to live outside the borders of conventional society were inspiring. It felt like I had arrived at a sacred shrine, and I was intent on taking a picture of the front of the markers, which sounds easier than it was. The graves are close to the road, with a sturdy hedge protecting the gravesite from the traffic. With bushes poking in my back and sandy pine needles gathering in my sandals, I struggled to capture the inscription: "Erected by the people of St. Helena in memory of Laura M. Towne. Entered into joy, St. Helena S.C. 1901. Their beloved and venerated teacher friend helper and physician for forty years."

Every pilgrimage has its rewards and its challenges. As we drove back to town, I felt satisfied with our visit to the island. I could feel myself falling in love with the area, with the Sea Islands. Their moist air and shady lanes were seeping into my soul. I was discovering the places that had nurtured my father. The mud in the creeks, the moldy smell, the dark brown faces, the tropical foliage, and the sound of cicadas had all shaped him from the time he was small. It would have felt like home to him, and it was beginning to feel that way to me.

* * *

The next morning, Sally and I walked among ominous remains of dead trees on the beach at Hunting Island State Park, as though wandering back in time. The enormous driftwood forms towered over us like the ribs of a ship wrecked on nearby shoals. Bleached by sun and water, they conjured up images of bones. *Bones*, I thought, *bones of the ancestors*. Thousands of African people were brought to that island against their will. By 1861, there were 12,000 African people living on St. Helena and its adjacent islands.

It was our last morning in Beaufort, and we had decided to go to the beach first thing, to Hunting Island State Park on the barrier island next to St. Helena. As we walked along, I marveled at the tropical vegetation, towering palms and stocky palmettos, that came right up to the edge of the broad flat expanse of hard-packed, fine-grained, white sand.

The beach sloped so gently that when we got in the calm water, we must have walked twenty-five yards before it even came up to our waists. We went out far enough to swim in the soft warm water. The waves were so gentle that it felt more like being in a gulf than an ocean. Looking back at the shore, a stout lighthouse, black on top with white below, rose above the graceful palms. It seemed like paradise. Perhaps it was, before my ancestors arrived. I wondered if the beaches of Tybee Island had looked like this when my father was growing up. The one I had seen looked more like the North Carolina beaches I knew: ribbons of road, lines of houses, beach grass, sand, and waves, though the sand at Tybee was fine and packed like Hunting Island.

We saw very few people, maybe half a dozen visitors and a couple of maintenance people. I asked a tourist to take a picture of Sally and me. In the photograph, we stand side by side in our bathing suits, the ocean to our back, our arms around each other's waist. I have dozens of pictures of us, at all different ages, standing just like that. In one of my favorites, Sally and I are on the patio of their house in Houston and appear to be wearing Easter dresses. A wide-brimmed hat shades Sally's face. We must have been visiting the Pattons when they lived in Texas. I was probably nine, and Sally might have been ten. Our parents helped us stay connected during those years. There are pictures of us at summer camp, at our weddings, and at our parents' houses in Tulsa. Since Sally hates the flash of a camera, I suggested years ago that we face each other instead of looking straight ahead. We have lots of pictures of the two of us in that pose. No flash was needed in the bright sun at Hunting Island, so we both squint straight at the camera.

Back in Beaufort, we showered, packed, and stopped at Gail and Bill's to say goodbye. Gail loaded me down with a shopping bag full of family papers to peruse, copy, and return. Then Sally and I drove back out to St. Helena for lunch at Gullah Grub. The restaurant, which took over an old country store, sits at the only substantial intersection on the island. We sat at a small table by the front windows and admired a collection of sea grass baskets displayed on the porch. While we waited for our food, I went outside to visit with the basketmaker. After eating a hearty stew, we wandered across the street to the Red Piano, a shop full of folk art and outsider art from around the South. I bought two tiny postcard-sized paintings as an attempt to take some of the Lowcountry home.

Twenty-Six
Jones Street
Savannah, 2008

Sally and I crossed the Savannah River into the city bearing the same name and found our way to the Eliza Thompson House, a small hotel at 5 West Jones Street, a shady lane in the historic district, just a block from my great-grandmother's house. It was late afternoon when we climbed the steps to the entrance of the inn. The front door was up a flight of stairs, because long ago the lower level would have been a cellar or stable. The tall windows of our room faced Jones Street and offered a fine view of trees and the quiet street below.

After dinner at a downtown restaurant, we went back to our room to check in on the Democratic National Convention. Earlier in the week Caroline Kennedy had said that Barack Obama was giving people hope the way her father had. I watched a tape of Michelle Obama's inspiring speech from the night before. I found she was as brilliant and stately as her husband. She had survived Princeton and Harvard, after all. How amazed her South Carolina ancestors would have been to see her on that convention stage.

The next morning, Sally and I ate breakfast in the inn's courtyard. The sky was clear and the temperature was so pleasant that I lingered at the table long enough to make some notes about how much I had enjoyed St. Helena the day before. As for Savannah, there were many things I wanted to see or learn, though I was vague on what they were. I was sure I wanted to see the house on Jones Street where my great-grandmother had lived.

Modern Savannah (population 130,000) sits on a forty-foot bluff above the river and is the fifth-largest container port in the

U.S. after Los Angeles, Long Beach, New York, and Charleston. I imagined my father sitting on the bluff watching ships on the river.

Sally and I agreed that a guided tour would be a good introduction to the city. As I settled into my seat atop the open-air trolley, I was eager to understand more of the personality and charm of my father's hometown.

Savannah is a beautiful and a lucky city, having been spared destruction on several occasions. Residents say that General Sherman found Savannah so delightful when he arrived with his troops in December 1864 that instead of leveling it, he gave it to President Lincoln as a Christmas gift. While that may be true, Savannah offered no resistance, and Sherman needed a place to regroup, one that could support his troops and the thousands of refugees from slavery that followed.

As the trolley pulled out of its parking lot, our tour guide pointed out that hurricane season runs from June through November, with August and September being the most likely months for storms. Lest we be nervous, she reassured us that the city had not taken a direct hit since 1979. While Savannah may have been a lucky city, it is also tucked into a protective curve in the coastline. As we rolled along, it occurred to me that my father shared some characteristics with his hometown—being attractive, charming, and lucky had served each of them well.

General James Oglethorpe, who founded Savannah in 1733, designed a city with twenty-four central squares. Though it took more than a century for residents to complete the building of the squares, our ninety-minute tour promised to visit them all. I wondered whether reciting the names of the squares had been a requirement for Savannah schoolchildren like my dad.

In Johnson Square, we saw Christ Episcopal Church, founded in 1733 and served by John Wesley in 1736 and 1737. In Wright Square, we passed the Lutheran Church of the Ascension, and I sensed that my grandmother had not been the only religious person in town.

In the early days, the squares were fenced for livestock, but now they are more likely to shelter tourists or provide attractive locations for movies. As we passed Chippewa Square, our guide pointed out the bench where Tom Hanks sat in *Forrest Gump*. The release of *Midnight in the Garden of Good and Evil*, known simply as "the movie" in Savannah, was responsible for a dramatic increase in the city's tourist trade. On Monterey Square, we admired the handsome Mercer House, where the film's murder took place, and we learned that the film's iconic Bird Girl statue now lives in a museum on Telfair Square.

Oaks and azaleas on Oglethorpe Avenue gave me an idea of how pretty 37th Street might have been when my father was growing up there. As we passed Leopold's Ice Cream, which began making old-fashioned ice cream in 1919, I wondered whether my father was ever allowed such a treat on a hot August day.

As we approached the river and Factors Row where the cotton brokers worked, our guide said that Savannah was once the number one cotton port. I imagined clerks recording numbers of bales and prices in heavy ledger books and thought of my grandfather, who came to Savannah in the early 1900s and found a job as a clerk in a fertilizer company. Bumping along the cobblestone street in front of "The Row," we learned that the stones had been used as ballast in ships that came from England in the 1850s. Instead of throwing them away, they were recycled as paving stones.

As our tour drew to a close, our guide cleared up one confusing thing for me. She said Spanish moss is not a parasite, it doesn't hurt the trees, and it isn't even Spanish.

* * *

The next morning, I walked a block to 116 West Jones Street, the house where my great-grandmother, Missouri Arrington, once lived. The 1910 census indicated that my grandparents were also living there with their new baby, my uncle Henry. The three-story brick house with black shutters was glued to its neighbors on either side. Just one room wide, upper rooms had only two windows facing the street. The sign in front said *Joseph's Salon*. As I approached the front door, I was surprised that it opened, revealing a man about my age. Though he was in a hurry, the man let me peek inside. "I have errands to run but I open at 10:00. Come back and I'll show you the house," he said as he closed the door and hurried off down the street.

My grandfather sold 116 W. Jones Street in 1965 for about $3,600. You'd have to add several zeros to buy the well-preserved nearly 200-year-old house now.

When I returned later that morning, the owner showed me around. The salon took up two lower levels, which he explained would have once been kitchen and servants' quarters. I followed the curving staircase up to the third floor of the house, admiring exposed brick walls and wondering how three generations of my family, and several boarders, all lived in the narrow rooms.

I left the house feeling satisfied. I had stood in the house where my grandmother and great-grandmother lived a hundred years before. Not only that, I was falling in love with the whole area.

I wasn't sure I wanted to love Georgia. If I could love Savannah, then I might have to stop blaming the state. I'd have to admit that it wasn't his birthplace that caused my father to run off in the middle of my growing up. Maybe Georgia wasn't all musty and backward and the people weren't all crazy. Of course there were crazy people, like my grandmother, and there was a wicked history of racial violence and discrimination, but those were not so different from Texas and Oklahoma. If I fell in love with Savannah, then I might have to admit it wasn't all Georgia's fault.

Twenty-Seven
Beautiful Beaufort by the Sea
2009

"See the best state on the best roads," Liz wrote in the visitors' log at the South Carolina Welcome Center on I-95. The saying, suggested by a South Carolina schoolchild, won a statewide contest when Liz's father was on the highway commission. We both agreed it was a better slogan than the current, "Smiling faces. Beautiful places." I walked out of the air-conditioned visitors' center, maps in hand, and into ninety-degree heat with ninety percent humidity. April already felt like summer, and I was glad to be traveling in Liz's new sky-blue Toyota Camry Hybrid. We could make the car as cold as we wanted and not feel guilty about burning up too much fossil fuel.

On this Saturday in late April 2009, we were headed for Liz's hometown of Beaufort, or as Liz liked to say, "Beautiful Beaufort by the sea, twenty-three miles from Yemasee." Shortly after a road sign announced, "Beaufort County," Liz turned left on a two-lane road that led into a tunnel of green. Overhead branches met and entangled as though closing off the space behind us. I shut my eyes, breathed in, and felt a sense of relief. I was exactly where I wanted to be.

We crossed the bridge onto Port Royal Island, which includes the town of Beaufort, and passed a sign for Seabrook, an unincorporated community off to the right. I remembered the sign from my previous visit and knew we were close. Liz turned left onto Bay Street, where grand antebellum houses to our left sat keeping watch over the bay.

"That's the house," Liz said, pointing to one of the big white houses. "Oh, my God," I gasped. She had said we would stay with her brother, leaving out the part about his living in a mansion. "That's why I never tell people about the house," said Liz.

She was eight when her parents bought the big house that had been damaged from Hurricane Gracie and began putting it back together. Liz wasn't crazy about living in a showpiece, but her brother Geddes had taken it on after their parents died—stripping it down to a simpler, somewhat more original form, exposing brick fireplaces, removing sheet rock from wood paneling, ripping up old carpeting, and restructuring part of the central curving staircase. I was dumbstruck as I anticipated entering the set for *Gone with the Wind*. "It's just a house," I kept telling myself.

We drove around to the back, a good thing since it was less impressive than the columned porch facing the bay. Perhaps I could get over being star-struck and act like a normal person. The garage at the back of the yard and the piles of bricks (just like the ones at my house) made it look less formal. Geddes came down the high divided back stairs to greet us.

Liz had also failed to mention how cute her brother is. Just under six feet, the man, near our age, offered a warm smile, a gentle hug to his sister, a welcoming handshake to me, and offered to help us into the house with our bags.

I was transported, as though arriving at the Ritz with a doorman offering to help me to the Presidential suite. I had pictured a well-used family home on a leafy backstreet in town. Since I knew her brother lived alone, I had even wondered whether it might be piled high with newspapers and magazines. I knew Geddes was an architect, but that didn't mean he was a good housekeeper.

The house, which announced its presence with authority, had been deconstructed and rebuilt over several years by the man who loved it. Even the half-circle of bricks at the base of the back stairs, which looked like it had been there since my grandmother was a girl, had been carefully designed to go with the age and style of the house. Geddes gave me slivers of old brick that had been sawed off in an attempt to make the pieces fit just right. "We got a little obsessive about the project," he admitted.

The inside of the house had a simple dignity. A collection of plain wooden chairs adorned the front hall, and the kitchen was small and cozy for a house of 4,500 square feet. Simple blinds hung at most of the over-sized windows. Quilts stitched by the beloved Ellen (the household employee when Liz was growing up) covered the beds. Once the heart and soul of the house, Ellen had slept in a room across from the kitchen at night.

My room on the second floor, probably eighteen by twenty feet with fifteen-foot ceilings, felt larger than my living room at home. Sparsely furnished, it had enough space for my yoga class to spread out on the floor. "I believe I require larger accommodations," I said to myself in my haughtiest voice. Three large windows with working sash ropes were open to the breeze from the bay.

I put on my walking shoes. After sitting in a car all afternoon, I needed to stretch my limbs and survey my new surroundings. Back down in the kitchen, Geddes was setting out cheese and crackers and offering libations. When I said I was going for a walk, he suggested, "Some people enjoy walking along the bay into town." Feeling slightly resistant, I went out the back door and took off in another direction. I didn't want a guide for this part. I wanted to explore my father's homeland in my own way.

As I wandered along the back streets the pavement was giving off the day's heat. When I finally made my way to Bay Street, I quickly learned a lesson known to every Lowcountry resident: it's cooler when you catch the breeze, and you are more likely to catch a breeze closer to the water. Plus the bay was nice to look at. OK, the guy who lived there knew which way to send the tourist. I conceded that round to my host.

Back at the house, I called my cousin Gail and arranged to meet her at ten o'clock the next morning at the Masonic Temple for the services of St. Mark's Chapel. Gail said the building looks like a Shinto shrine. I told her I'd have Liz and Geddes with me, and she suggested we all have lunch afterward.

Liz had invited Julie, an old friend, to join us for dinner on Saturday evening. We had brought bread, wine, and greens from North Carolina; Geddes had gotten some fish; and Julie brought dessert. A feast was had in the large dining room, which was home to three dining room tables, two breakfronts, and a plethora of chairs. We sat around a dark square wooden table in the middle of the room and enjoyed shad cooked in butter according to the Lowcountry Bible on cooking, the *Charleston Receipts*. So happily comfortable together, we listened to stories of the house and "the old days" in Beaufort until we all looked like we were falling asleep. Julie tore herself away, and the rest of us went to bed.

* * *

On Sunday morning, I dressed for church and went downstairs to cut up strawberries I had brought for my customary bowl of yogurt and granola. *Squirt!* Strawberry juice spewed on the front of my white shirt. I ran upstairs, washed the shirt in the sink, put on a black one, returned to the kitchen, and tucked a kitchen towel in the neckline before slicing any more berries. I settled myself at the square dining room table again, staring out the windows that faced the bay.

Geddes joined me at the table long enough for me to capture his full name and address in my journal before it was time to go. Intent on taking a picture of the bay, I persuaded Liz and Geddes to follow me outside. I snapped pictures of the siblings, the bay, and the front of the house, obscured by palmettos and two very large evergreens, which had once been family Christmas trees.

We left for church later than we had planned, but nothing in Beaufort is very far away.

As we settled into the large windowless room at the Masonic Temple, I found myself wishing for a space that brought the beautiful landscape into the service of worship. St. Mark's was celebrating its sixth anniversary that week, and people seemed happy to have left the motel where they had met for several years. On my previous trip, there had been only eighteen in the congregation. This time I counted thirty-four. Perhaps they would grow large enough to afford a building with windows some day.

We three visitors sat in theater style chairs against the wall. Others sat in movable chairs in front of us. A red sea of carpet spread across the room to Gail at the piano in the opposite corner. I noticed a considerable amount of gray hair, which made this congregation just like many others in America today.

I settled into my unfamiliar surroundings and tolerated the Episcopal service. The Presbyterian in me has never understood why they want to say the same words over and over, but I enjoyed hearing Gail play the piano, and the service ended soon enough. I found the priest and parishioners warm and friendly and shared their joy at having six or eight visitors that day. They were clearly providing a much-needed alternative to the conservative parish downtown.

Gail, Bill, Liz, Geddes, and I had lunch on the deck of a restaurant right on the river near the Lady's Island Bridge. When Geddes asked Gail about her first memory of me, she told the story of my being the flower girl in her wedding when I was four. She also described visiting my parents in Dallas in 1945 before I was born. Mother and Daddy had been married for only a year when Grandmother Stokes took Gail on a train trip from Georgia to California, with visits to friends and family all along the way. Daddy had finished his residency at Parkland and was teaching in Dallas and was still working at the hospital. "The hospital where John Kennedy was taken," Gail added. I had never made the connection that my father worked in the hospital that would later receive the body of our dead president. I never made the connection because I was too busy connecting up the fact that in the wintry months of 1963–64, the President was shot, and my father left my mother (and me). Those were the only historical facts that interested me as a twelve-year-old.

Later Gail showed me a scrapbook of the trip. When I admired a picture of Daddy in his medical whites and a postcard that mentioned her visit to Grandview, my mother's hometown, she pulled them right out and gave them to me. I held the items in my hands like puzzle pieces wondering how they fit the picture I was trying to create.

As lunch continued, Gail and I told stories about our grandfather. He was an acrobat in the circus before he was married and loved to kid around and entertain his grandchildren. "I can count to 100 faster than you can," he'd say. "Ten, ten, double ten, forty-five, fifteen." I could see the people around the table doing the math in their heads, "ten plus ten is...." He also liked to bet on the horses, a fact he hid from Grandmother. He passed on to my father some of his talents for entertaining others and for sneaking around.

Granddad moved to Oklahoma after Grandmother died and lived with Daddy, Faye, and their children on a lake near Manford, forty-five minutes from Tulsa. According to Gail, Daddy would take Granddad to the pool hall in Manford and leave him. The elderly man would sit by the door, like a frog just waiting for a fly. Some young dude would come in and say, "Gramps, wanna play?" Thinking he'd pick up some easy money, the dude would add, "Wanna bet a little?" My grandfather would wipe the floor or, in this case, the pool table with these young upstarts. In Savannah he had played pool secretly, because Grandmother didn't approve of betting, playing cards, or much of anything that might be construed as fun. But in Oklahoma, Granddad got to be as wild as an octogenarian could be.

A light breeze mingled with the affable lunchtime conversation as Gail wandered into another story. She said that one time after a visit to our grandparents, my cousin Sharon was in the backseat of the family car when her father came out of Grandmother's house all upset. He got in the car and blurted out that both Grandmother and Granddad had been married before they got married to each other. I already knew about Granddaddy and even had a copy of his handwritten story about being married and divorced when he was young, but this information about Grandmother was news to me. I was divorced, as were my parents and my father's parents, though not from each other. And Grandmother's father had gone off traveling with his whirligig.

Geddes asked Gail and Bill if they could tell us the secret to a happy marriage. Good question, since all of us at the table had been divorced except Liz. "Get rid of the junk early. The psychological junk," they said. With that bit of wisdom, we said goodbye and went back to the house on Bay Street for a nap.

* * *

Liz and I picked Julie up later that afternoon, and we all drove out to St. Helena Island to visit the garden Geddes had planted at a friend's house. The friend had worked the garden beside the sound for several years, but this year it was a joint effort. Geddes was there watering rows of vegetables, newly planted in dark earth. He explained that adding topsoil and compost to the native sand made for good soil. I was surprised to find palmetto trees growing in the midst of tiny vegetables and took lots of pictures of the unusual garden by the sea.

From there we drove to Coffin Point to visit Liz's friend who lives there. I had seen the big house on my tour with Mr. Middleton the year before and was eager to go inside. The gracious old house had been carefully restored but not overdone. I was beginning to see a trend. There was a relaxed Lowcountry feel to these houses, in town and in the country, markedly different from their prissy city cousins in Charleston and Savannah. After a stroll to the water's edge, we settled at the kitchen table. I drank lime soda while the other three women discussed children and local politics. Cotton voile curtains hung from ceiling to floor at open windows in nearby rooms, and the whole house seemed to be breathing as the light curtains billowed and fell still.

When Liz and I returned to the house on Bay Street, all I wanted to do was sit on the front porch, feel the breeze on my skin, smell the air, and stare out at the water across the street. As I sat, I gazed at sailboats anchored quietly on the blue water beyond the marsh grasses. Geddes had said that when he and his father had looked out on the bay, his dad always asked which way the tide was going. I wondered, if I sat there long enough, whether I would ever come to understand the rhythm of the tide that slowly turned the boats this way and that.

Twenty-Eight
Penn Center
2009

Liz and I sat in mismatched chairs at a well-worn table in Ada McKenzie's office at the Penn Center. Except for the young museum curator's computer on a desk against one wall, the plain room still resembled the school office or classroom it had been. Ada had welcomed us to her simple office for a chat when we returned to St. Helena the next morning.

It didn't take us long to discover that Ada was from Massachusetts and that her mother had been at Smith College when I was. Ada had a degree in African Caribbean studies with a concentration in religion, so we spoke of books we had read on religion, race, and the South. We both knew Edward Ball's *Slaves in the Family*, which follows the descendants of black people who were enslaved on the Ball family's South Carolina plantations.

I was fascinated by Ada's comments about how far the local culture had spread in the Gullah Diaspora. Some people from the Sea Islands escaped to Florida and became part of the Seminole Nation. A lot of Black Seminoles wound up in Oklahoma, and a few eventually migrated to Texas. There is a small town in Texas where Gullah is still spoken today. I had not expected to find such connections with the Southwest there on St. Helena.

We discussed the missionaries who came to the South in the 1860s, the schools they started, and how many schools were started by women. Penn Center, which began in 1862, was the first such school. I asked lots of questions about Laura Towne and Ellen Murray, the Penn Center's founders.

The community's memory of Laura and Ellen is complicated. Penn handed out diplomas for the last time in 1948. Many of the older graduates revere the women and the education they received from the school. After the school closed and interest in Gullah culture began to grow, there was disagreement. Some felt that the white American education they had received was better than the old ways; others disagreed.

Laura and Ellen, like so many of the missionaries from the North, were patriarchal in their approach, at least at first, as if they were trying to turn their students into good New Englanders. Some of Laura's language in the early pages of her diary is offensive, but her attitude toward the people of St. Helena became more respectful as time went on.

After visiting with Ada, we wandered through the museum displays, and Liz read signs aloud to me in Gullah.

One photograph of philanthropist George Foster Peabody, at a meeting of Penn trustees at his office in New York in 1902, reminded me that white northern men were overseeing the school at that time. Today, the center seems to be in the hands of African Americans, many of them native to the island.

Back out in the lobby, I lost myself in a sea of white fabric, long flowing strips an artist had suspended from the ceiling. The sea of fabric carried me back to a different place and time. As a tiny child, I had gazed in awe at endless tablecloths pouring off the ironing boards of the two black women who worked in my grandmother's modest kitchen in Texas. Inez and Juanita were like goddesses to me, protectors of the hearth and artisans who turned rumpled cloth into smooth perfection. The exhibit was meant to suggest aprons once worn by Lowcountry midwives, but standing there staring at the flowing white strips, I was lost in another world.

* * *

The next morning, I went out for a walk before breakfast. When I returned, I stopped to count the boats in the bay. There were seventeen. On my way into the yard, I slammed the gate, and

Geddes must have heard me. By the time I reached the porch, he had swung open the screen door and was saying, "Welcome home." That was it. He had named it. I felt at home in that place, in that watery landscape of my father's birth.

Twenty-Nine
My Sister the Chimp
2010

When people ask me if I have siblings, I hesitate and usually say, "Yes, and no." I experience myself as an only child, because I am the only child my mother and father had together, and I was the only child either of them had for many years. The summer I turned fourteen, my father and his second wife had a daughter. The next year my mother remarried, and six-year-old Bonnie came along in the deal. In the next few years, my father and Faye increased their family with a son, a second daughter, and a baby chimpanzee.

By the time I get through explaining all that, the person who asked the question has no idea where to focus or what to say. The most common reaction of the questioner is to tilt her head and let her mouth drop slightly open. I often say, "Haven't I told you that?" And then I wonder, "Which part haven't I mentioned, the part about the siblings or about the chimp?"

One weekend in February 2010, while looking at a snapshot of my father and his second family, I started thinking about Bessie and wondered whether there might be anything about her on the web. When I googled my father's name along with the word *chimp*, I was unprepared for what I found: a chapter in a book that mentioned them both. What was startling was that the book wasn't about my father or about chimpanzees. *Daniel Webster's 52 Kids* was about the 1952 graduating class from Tulsa's Daniel Webster High School, which included my stepmother Faye. For their fiftieth reunion, Donna J. Wilson interviewed her classmates and published their stories, sections of which were available online. The chapter about Faye included a section about Bessie and reminded me that the little chimp had died of a brain tumor when she was about seven years old. The book also mentioned that Jane Goodall had come to see Bessie at my dad's house. I couldn't believe there was a book with a chapter about my stepmother. I always thought my father and the chimp were the ones worth writing about.

It had always made perfectly good sense to me that my father adopted a chimp. We had birds and fish and cats and dogs, and after he married Faye, he had more house pets and eventually horses. I knew the chimp. I spent the night with my father and his second family every now and then, but I was so focused on how weird it was that my father lived with these other people that it never once occurred to me the unusual part was that he was raising a chimpanzee.

The *Daniel Webster* book reported that Bessie came to live with Daddy and Faye via a program at the University of Oklahoma, that she sat on the counter while Faye cooked dinner, and that she only lived to be about seven. (It is not unusual for chimps to live to be forty years old.)

Of even greater interest was Faye's version of meeting my father and of their subsequent life together. She said she met Malcolm in Las Vegas in 1963, though she neglected to mention that he was married to my mother at the time. The book says they married, moved to a lake house, and had three children. It also describes their time at the lake as idyllic. Though I didn't visit them often, I would never have described life with my alcoholic father, three small children, my elderly grandfather, and a chimp that way. The book also says that after Daddy died in 1976, Faye fell in love with a Denver oilman and married him in 1978. As I recall, she and my dad were divorced, and they were both remarried before Daddy died. Though the sequence of events doesn't match my memory exactly, she was married to my father all the same. After Faye divorced my father, she married again and moved to Colorado with the three children and no chimp.

Years later when Jane Goodall was in Durham for a lecture and I had a chance to speak with her, I asked if she might have ever visited Bessie the chimp. "Very likely," she replied. I was amazed that my stepmother had probably been telling the truth about the famous chimpanzee expert. It wouldn't have surprised me if she had made it up.

I couldn't get over the fact that my stepmother was the one who showed up in a book. I had always thought of her as the woman who stole my father. Perhaps it was worth noting that she was a female pilot in the 1960s and that she raised a chimp.

* * *

A couple of days after I found the book that mentioned Bessie the chimp, I was packing my bags to go to the beach for an RCWMS-sponsored art workshop with Sue Sneddon. The workshop would be Thursday–Sunday, but I was going early, on Tuesday, to help Sue set up and to have some extra days at the coast. I stopped at Whole Foods in Raleigh mid-afternoon to get something to eat. Once inside, I noticed Lao, a Durham friend, at one of the café tables. Dressed in a suit, she looked as though she might have been lobbying at the legislature but reported she had just come from a meeting. She has been a criminal justice advocate for thirty years. Though she had finished eating, she suggested I get some food and join her.

Lao and I caught up while I enjoyed my green beans, sweet potatoes, and tube-shaped pasta. I remembered to ask her about her younger sister, who had been ill. Lao said the sister was getting along well enough after having a brain tumor removed and that she would be back at Duke again soon to see her doctor. Lao lamented the fact that her sister still had to work full-time. When I asked what kind of work she did, Lao said this sister worked with apes, just like their older sister. They were both in Iowa at a foundation dedicated to great apes. The sister who had been ill was one of a handful of humans who could hang out with the apes in their enclosure and not worry about being injured. She had known most of them as babies. Lao said that when her sister showed the apes the surgical scar on her head, they touched it tenderly. Sometimes she would lie down and take a nap with the apes. Both of Lao's sisters are interested in the language ability and the culture of the primates with whom they work.

That's when I mentioned that my father had adopted a baby chimp to raise along with his infant son. "Really!" Lao's eyes got big. I explained that it was part of some experiment at the University of Oklahoma. Lao countered that her sister got her Ph.D. from the University of Oklahoma. I said the chimp's name was Bessie and I thought she was born around 1968. Lao did some quick calculations and said, "I think that's when my sister was at O.U." *Oh my God!* I thought. It was happening again. From out of nowhere, here came a piece of information connected to my search for my father. I've known Lao for well over thirty years, but we had never stumbled on this connection. As Lao put it, "I've got chimp cousins and you have a chimp sister."

* * *

I pulled out of the grocery parking lot still stunned by my good fortune. I actually knew someone whose sister might know about the program at O.U. and now suspected there might be information about it on the Internet. I was still headed to the art workshop with Sue Sneddon and drove all the way thinking about people who worked with chimpanzees.

When I crossed the bridge onto Emerald Isle, the sun had already set, but there was still a stripe of deep pink just above the western horizon. The water was a deep blue-grey, and the edges of the small grassy islands had a pinkish glow. At low tide, the wet sand at the edge of the islands reflects the color in the sky. I had never noticed anything quite like it before. It was a Sue Sneddon moment, I thought as I drove onto Emerald Isle. Sue had taught me to notice things like the colors on the water at sunset. It was one of the things I liked about hanging out with an artist.

Wednesday dawned bright and cold. I got up, put on my blue bathrobe, ate breakfast, and set up my painting table while Sue set up for the workshop. After lunch, while Sue was out hunting for light bulbs and a folding table, I piled up on the sofa in a small warm room in our large borrowed house and went hunting on the Internet. It took me less than five minutes to locate stories about Dr. Bill Lemmon, the "wacky" psychologist at the University of

Oklahoma who wore sandals and a goatee, bred chimps, and placed them in human families.

It was an experimental time, and Lemmon became interested in the sexual arousal of female chimpanzees. I'm not sure which part of his personality, his research, or his activities led to the closing of his research center, but by 1982 it was out of business.

I found articles by Lao's older sister whose research interests suggested she might have studied with Lemmon. It appeared that the sister had continued some of the work started by Lemmon, in a less sensational way. She worked at Georgia State University for thirty years and then at the Great Ape Trust in Iowa.

Bessie was not just one chimp adopted by one family in Oklahoma; she was part of a much larger research project; and it seemed likely that Jane Goodall had visited her at my father's house. What good fortune to have run into Lao and made the connection about the chimps!

Thinking I was having a lucky day, I decided to try one more time to locate some of Daddy and Faye's children, my siblings. A couple of years before, I had gotten far enough to figure out that Faye had changed the children's last name after she married again and my father had died just two or three years later. Never able to locate a Tim Stokes, I had looked for my brother with Faye's new last name and had found such a person. That's as far as I had gotten. I was more than a little nervous about whether my father's other children would want to have contact with me and how they might have turned out. They were, after all, the products of alcoholism and divorce just like I was, and what if they were all sort of messed up?

That Wednesday afternoon at the beach, I felt brave enough to find out and thought of trying Facebook. I had been using Facebook for about a year and was amazed at how many old friends I had been able to locate. I typed in Tim's name and up he popped. You can't find out much about most people if you aren't "friends" with them, but he looked like an average white guy and appeared to be the right age. I scrolled through his friends, and there was the older of his sisters, Delisa. I clicked on her name, and up popped a gorgeous picture of her standing beside a horse. She looked confident, happy, and beautiful, with her mother's winning smile and my father's compact agile body.

With just a bit more research on the Internet, I discovered she had married into a wealthy Denver family and that she and her husband supported the arts. Her life certainly didn't sound messed up. She had been a competitive skier, was a horsewoman, was married, had three children, and lived in Colorado.

That's when it hit me. Bonnie had just moved to Colorado Springs, which meant I had *four* siblings in Colorado. My head was about to fly apart again.

When Sue returned to the beach house in the late afternoon, I was still sitting on the sofa in my blue bathrobe. I was so absorbed in finding pieces of my past that I had forgotten to eat lunch. I could barely get the words out, "My father adopted a chimp and I found my half-siblings!"

How is it that I have three "halves" I've known nothing about for the last thirty-five years? Whose responsibility was it to connect me to them? My father was dead. It was certainly not my mother's or my stepmother's. I guess it was ours, and until recently I had not known how to find them. In fact, I had felt slightly unsettled when I thought of trying to find them. But those days were over. I had located them on Facebook. I wondered when I would be brave enough to push the "friend" button or to send a message?

I decided that I'd wait a couple of weeks, until the end of February. Since Daddy died February 29, 1976, most years I marked that anniversary on the 28th. When the last day of February rolled around in 2010, it was also the full moon, which made the day seem even more significant. My father had been dead for thirty-four years. It felt like the right day to try to contact my lost siblings. I drafted a Facebook message.

2/28/10
Subject: Our father Malcolm

Delisa,

I've looked for you several times, on the Internet, over the years, but found no clues. Last week, I stumbled on you on Facebook. The wonders of modern technology! As I've thought about you for the last week or so, I've been getting up my courage to contact you. Once Daddy died, our mothers did nothing to try to connect us. As the years went by, when I thought about it, I usually stumbled on where to begin. From the picture, you look healthy and like you still live in Colorado.

I'm in North Carolina where I've been since 1973. I only saw Daddy a little bit between 1973 and the time he died in 1976. It took me decades to get over being mad at him for leaving and then dying. In the last ten years I've enjoyed sweet memories of him and have been doing some research on him. I have (and you and Kelly and Tim have) first cousins in Georgia. Three of the 4 of them are still alive and they now send me things. I have a set of letters our father wrote to his brother when he was in medical training.

I'm sorry it has taken me so long to reach out to you. I can't know whether you will welcome this contact. I hope that you and all of your family are well.

Jeanette Stokes

I sent the message mid-day on Sunday, February 28, 2010. That evening, I had a message back from Kelly, the younger of the two sisters.

2/28/10, 9:44 pm

Jeanette—We (Delisa and I) are so excited to hear from you! This is your little sister Kelly. WOW. I have always known about you and Delisa and I have even looked for you. We just were spelling your name wrong!

Kelly went on to say she was having computer trouble and to call one of them and gave me their numbers. I sent a return message saying, "This is better than I had imagined. I got both of you at once!" and picked up my cell phone and dialed Kelly's number.

A cheerful voice answered, "Hello." "This is your sister, Jeanette," I said. We spent the next few minutes squealing and repeating, "I can't believe it. This is so amazing." Kelly explained that Delisa was driving in a snowstorm; well, her husband was driving. She had picked up my Facebook message on her phone and asked Kelly to get into her Facebook account to check and see if it was really me. That's when Kelly sent me the message.

I learned right away that Kelly was 41, Delisa was 44, and Tim was 42. The sisters had four boys and a girl between them, and Tim was single. Kelly said that they all thought the nine-year-old girl looked like me. "You and your husband have to come see us," she insisted, saying we should stay with her sister, because Delisa had a great big house and more money than God.

I called Delisa and tried to imagine her on a Colorado mountain road in the snow. We spoke briefly, and she explained that she and her family were leaving the next day for Indonesia and Thailand. I mentioned that our father had been in Burma, Thailand, Hong Kong, and Japan in 1957. He would have loved that she traveled a lot.

Late that evening, after I talked with my sisters, I e-mailed my Georgia cousins to let them know about their cousins in Colorado. I mentioned that Faye was seventy-five years old and that she had five grandchildren. I also reminded them about the chimp. My cousins all responded, were delighted with the news, and remembered about the chimp.

Beth said she remembered that Faye was once a candidate to be an astronaut, or something like that, and that she was very smart. Beth met her in 1964 when she accompanied Daddy and Faye to the NY World's Fair and then had dinner with them afterward in "the village." She only saw Faye one other time, when she went to see them at their house outside Tulsa in 1970. She had just returned to the U.S. from two years in Morocco and wanted her Uncle Malcolm to meet her baby son. She met Daddy and Faye's children on that visit.

Gail took her children to Tulsa a couple of times to visit Daddy and Faye. She remembered they lived in a trailer at the lake while they were building their house. Sharon never met Faye or the children.

I learned one other interesting thing that day. In talking with Kelly, I discovered that Faye had taken all three of the children to our father's funeral. Kelly said she remembered a lot of wailing at the funeral, that Daddy's third wife was wailing and that Faye was crying. Kelly remembered how much she hated to see her mother cry. I didn't think I knew anyone who had been at my father's funeral. My aunt and uncle who had attended were now both gone. I wasn't sure why it mattered, but I was really happy to have discovered that my long-lost siblings had been there.

Thirty
Meeting My Siblings
Colorado, 2010

Dwight and I planned a trip to the Southwest in August 2010 so I could meet my half-siblings, whom I had not seen in over thirty-five years. I had no idea what to expect of my father's other children. I was nervous. Delisa had invited us to stay at her house. I knew almost nothing about her except that she lived in a big house and collected art. She had said she'd invite Kelly and Tim to come for dinner. I wondered whether my siblings would look or act like me and whether we would like one another.

The first stop was New Mexico, where we helped Sally Patton celebrate her sixtieth birthday. A friend who felt like a sister, Sally had been in my life for as long as I could remember. After a weekend near Abiquiu, with lots of good food and conversation, we left Sally and headed north.

Once over the state line in Colorado, Dwight and I turned east to follow a river and a narrow-gauge railroad and were delighted when we caught up with a small steam-driven, coal-fed train. We stopped to take pictures, and I called my stepfather, a railroad enthusiast, so he could hear the train huff and puff and blow its whistle. Talking with him reminded me that I had years of experience trying to make family with people to whom I wasn't actually related. How hard could it be to make a connection with people who were actual blood relatives?

Dwight and I sped through the board-flat, 150-mile-long San Luis Valley, past enormous sand dunes piled up against the Sangre de Cristo Mountains to the east, and then turned east again through the startling red gorge cut by the Arkansas River. The rushing river bore little resemblance to the wide mud flats of the Arkansas as I had known it in Tulsa. The next day, we made a quick stop in Colorado Springs to see my stepsister Bonnie. She and her husband had moved to Colorado the year before so their ten-year-old daughter could participate in a gymnastics program. As much as I enjoyed seeing Bonnie, I was aware that this was yet another sibling from whom I felt somewhat distant. Bonnie and I had lived in the same house while I was in high school and still liked one another, but she was nine years younger, and we had never been as close as either one of us might have liked.

When we arrived in Denver late that afternoon, I was feeling a bit anxious. My stomach was tight, and I was giving Dwight way too many driving instructions. Delisa's house was easy to find, just off a main road. As we pulled our small gray rental car up to an iron gate, I gasped. In front of us stood an enormous Mediterranean-style mansion. Now, this was my dad's kind of house—big and splashy with room for lots of people! Dwight pushed a call button on the keypad by the gate, and a nice voice said, "I'll meet you at the front door." The gate swung open, we drove through and parked on the circular drive in front of the house.

The "front door" was ten feet high and suitable for a medieval castle. I didn't see a doorbell, nor did I attempt to tug on the handle the size of a baseball bat. I just stood there staring at the hammered bronze door until it finally opened, revealing an enormous entry hall and a cheerful young woman who stuck out her hand and said, "Hi, I'm Jenny, Delisa's assistant." ("Wow," I thought, "I could sure use one of those!") Right behind Jenny I was surprised to see vivacious, redheaded Kelly, the younger of my two half-sisters. As we hugged, I searched for anything I could remember about her as a child, but all I recalled was her darling red hair. Kelly announced that Delisa was in the shower. ("Running late," I thought, "a family trait.")

My heart was beating a little fast as I tried to hold all the feelings zinging around inside me. My chest felt tight and I kept needing to swallow. I asked for a restroom so I might calm down, but once inside, I tried to get my bearings. What did I want? What had I expected? Kelly seemed warm and funny. I liked her immediately.

She was small and agile like our father. As I stared at myself in the bathroom mirror, I tried to decide whether we looked related. I didn't feel very related. Kelly had her mother's flashing smile, which I found unnerving. I didn't like being reminded of my father's second wife, the woman who had carried my father away. Taking a deep breath, I opened the bathroom door prepared to meet all these new people, but there was no one in sight.

I wandered through cavernous spaces looking for the others. Eight large Andy Warhol prints of Mick Jagger hung on the walls. The highly polished floors were probably marble. Kelly had said her sister had more money than God, and now I believed her. I found everyone in a great room at the back of the house where floor-to-ceiling windows looked out on a patio. Dwight, Kelly, Jenny, and McKenzie, the children's nanny, were chatting. I didn't pay much attention to what they were saying, as I was distracted by my surroundings. Someone offered me something to drink, and I tried not to gape as I glanced around.

The C-shaped villa was built around a courtyard with a small garden. Large green umbrellas shaded a few tables and invited the visitor outdoors. Beyond were the pool and an open lawn, which, I later learned, could accommodate the landing of a helicopter. The open rooms reminded me of the house Daddy built when I was eight, only this one was much bigger. He would have thought this the perfect house for a large party. The great room held a sitting area, an eating area, and a spacious kitchen that would have delighted a commercial chef.

Kelly's two young sons emerged from somewhere, and Delisa appeared wearing snug black shorts and a fitted top, reminding me of her mother, who had exuded a kind of physicality men seemed to like. My mother had always dressed in attractive but somewhat modest clothing and had passed that sensibility on to me. I had already guessed from the Facebook pictures I had seen of my sisters that they picked up their mother's ability to be a mother and wear fetching clothing at the same time. Delisa's twins and her daughter Alexandra appeared, and then Kelly's husband Rick, and finally Tim. Tony, Delisa's husband, had flown to Napa for the day to discuss oil and wine and would return later in the evening.

I stared at the people, as though viewing abstract modern art, unable to interpret my own feelings or the effect the scene was having on me. What did any of this have to do with me? I had a strange sensation of leaving the room without leaving my body. Vague memories appeared in my fuzzy brain, memories of uncomfortable visits to my father's house when Kelly, Tim, and Delisa were small. I wondered whether I had felt as disoriented all those years ago.

Delisa offered to take Dwight and me on a tour of the house. The music room beside the great room was as big as a ballroom. It contained the baby grand piano Daddy bought after he married Faye, as well as a larger-than-life-size portrait of Marilyn Monroe. Delisa said it was the last picture taken of Monroe. The Internet later confirmed it was taken by well-known fine arts photographer Bert Stern during Monroe's last formal sitting. In a black dress with long sleeves, Monroe rests one cheek against her right hand and gazes downward, away from the camera.

The lighting system fascinated me. Each room had a panel of buttons that controlled its lights, while other panels in strategic locations controlled the lights all over the house. I had a child's instinct to start pressing buttons randomly just to see what would happen.

We went downstairs to an enormous "game room," with a wall-size screen for movies and sporting events, a bar, a pool table, and the stuffed heads of wild game our hosts had shot in Africa. Ten or twelve of them. *Bambi!* the voice inside my head yelled as I smiled and nodded. A full zebra-skin rug lay on the floor. "This, too?" I asked. Delisa nodded. *Oh, no, the zebra, too!* I directed my attention to an interesting faucet in the powder room and a small screen over the urinal, which allowed sports enthusiasts to drink plenty of beer and not miss a play.

A locked room stored art not on display upstairs and a bank safe that held high-powered rifles. I said nothing about my views on gun control. At least the arsenal was locked up.

Delisa had created ingenious play spaces for the children under the staircases. One contained costumes, another housed miniature buildings and plastic action figures. Upstairs, Alexandra had a room overlooking the courtyard. The twins have a wing with a playroom, bathroom, and two bedrooms, while their parents have a wing with bathrooms, dressing rooms, and a huge bedroom. Everything in the house was oversized, but simple, elegant, and open in design. I looked around for a cozy place one might settle to read a book and decided the occupants must read in bed.

Eventually we gathered in Delisa's enormous dining room. (I'm running out of synonyms for *big*.) Twelve of us sat around a large rectangle made of three smaller square tables. An ingenious and flexible system, I thought. Other adults managed the kids so I could visit with my sisters.

Dinner included chicken smothered in mushrooms and a lovely salad. I'm a vegetarian, so I ate lots of salad. Kelly must have noticed, because she asked if I wanted to give the rest of my chicken to her husband. There was macaroni and cheese with ground meat on top, mostly for the kids. I assumed the meat was beef until someone pointed out that it was elk meat from Delisa and Tony's ranch in the mountains. The older children were polite and helped by clearing the plates when we were finished eating. Kelly's little ones got squirmy, so someone spirited them away. Then we took lots of pictures of the siblings, which I hoped to study later for clues of family resemblances.

The evening was friendly and as relaxed as meeting new relatives could have been for any of us. Kelly and Delisa sat at the table with Dwight and me for a time, as we edged our way into family stories, comparing notes about how my father and their mother got together. The sisters knew that Daddy and Faye had gotten together before he and Mother were separated. The new and disturbing thing I learned was that my father kept on having affairs even after he married Faye.

That surprised me. I had always imagined my father being blissfully happy with his sexy girlfriend who became his young wife. I briefly imagined her fury when she realized she had gone from being the object of my father's desire to being a housewife and mother.

Then the kids needed attention. Alexandra had homework questions; the twins needed to go to sleep; and Kelly's little ones were tired and cranky. As Kelly's husband Rick strapped the little boys into car seats, I noticed how good my brother Tim was with them. The youngest boy was red-faced and screaming. When Tim spoke to him, the little guy quieted right down. When I asked, Tim said children often respond to him that way and wished our father had been that patient with children. If a few funny faces hadn't calmed a child, I couldn't imagine Daddy having the patience to keep trying.

Eventually Dwight and I sat down in the great room with my newly located siblings and told more stories. We three sisters compared our small frames as Tim wondered how he got to be such a big guy. My siblings referred to our father as Malcolm, since "Dad" was their mother's husband who had adopted them. We established that Daddy and Faye got married in a rush, that he continued to have affairs, and that the threats and loud arguments worried the children when they were little. Tired and satisfied that we had told enough stories, we agreed to give up the evening. Kelly and Tim went home. Tony returned from Napa with a case of wine, and we chatted with him for a bit. It was easy to see why my sister had fallen for him. Short, dark, attractive, and clearly in charge, he resembled a young Al Pacino. Something about his size and presence reminded me of our father.

On our last morning in Denver, Delisa got out the reels of film she had found at her mother's house a few months before. She had gone to the trouble of having the five reels put onto DVDs and wanted us to look at them together. As I ate my yogurt and granola, she put the first one in, and I knew immediately that she had found the movies of my father's trip around the world in 1957. There he was, standing before us in Kabul, Afghanistan, and there were the sheep crossing the only paved road in town, just as my mother had described. I could hardly believe my eyes. There he was waving and being silly on the screen just as I remembered. They were home movie quality; the scenes changed too quickly;

and he always panned across the landscape too fast. "Slow down!" I pleaded aloud as cathedrals and government buildings whizzed by. But never mind the quality, they were my father's movies. I felt I could almost touch him. I might have dissolved into a puddle of gratitude and affection, but I had to eat my cereal and finish packing or we'd be late to the airport. Before we left, Delisa packed up the film reels and a set of the DVDs for me to take home.

All I could think to say was, "Thank you, thank you." I was almost speechless in the face of this remarkable gift. How many times had Mother and I said we were sorry those movies had gotten away? It felt as though I had found some missing piece in a puzzle. I had set out on a quest five years before, to see what I could find out about my father and had picked up pieces of my father at every turn. My Georgia cousins had sent me letters and pictures and told me stories. My mother had kindly filled in lots of details. And my own sister had given me my father's movies of the world.

As we drove to the Denver airport, I noticed that much of the longing inside me had subsided. What I had found seemed to be enough.

Epilog
2010

I don't like everything I found out about my father. I still have to hike up my proverbial pant legs and step over the yucky stuff, such as his extra-marital affairs, but I've gotten better at tolerating the uncomfortable parts. I seem able to hold it all without any of it feeling too sad, too scary, or too overwhelming for me.

Labor Day 2010 fell just a few days after our return from Colorado. I spent part of the day washing the porch that stretches across the front of our house. I scrubbed and rinsed off years of accumulated dust until the pale yellow clapboard glowed. The next morning, I sat in one of the porch rockers, admired my clean surroundings, and wrote in my journal. I was on the very last page of a red journal I had purchased in Paris the Spring before and had taken to Colorado with me.

A woman in a green shirt parked on the street in front of my house, got out of her car, and helped a little boy out of the backseat. As they walked through the park next to my house, I could see the woman was talking on a cell phone. In that moment, I had an almost overwhelming urge to pick up a phone and call my father. It was a familiar feeling that I'd been having for most of my adult life. For so many years, that impulse to reach him had led only to silence. He was dead and gone so far away from me. But that day on the porch, he didn't seem quite so far away. When I called him to mind, he came with a sweet smile and a gentle hand on mine.

My father is no longer flying somewhere overhead; he's here with me, here in the letters and pictures, in the memories and stories, here in my heart.

Acknowledgements

Many thanks to everyone who has ever listened to me talk about this book project, anyone who has been in a writing group where I've read from earlier versions, and all the kind folks who have read pages. I used to think writing was a solo activity. I seem to require a whole posse of friends to make the journey from idea to the printed page and make it come alive.

I am so grateful to three of my Georgia cousins, Gail Stokes Hodsdon, Beth Stokes Clinton, Sharon Stokes Kilfeather, who knew my father as a young man and shared him with me in stories and letters.

Over the years, my mother has patiently answered my questions about my father and has tried to keep her own opinions somewhat to herself. I offer love and gratitude to her for her part in my search to understand my dad.

I am grateful to my long-lost siblings in Colorado who received me with such warmth and hospitality. Delisa, Kelly, and Tim, you are the best! I offer special thanks to Delisa for saving and reproducing some of our father's movies.

Peggy Payne helped to direct the development of the manuscript. You would think I'd learn to spot the boring, vague, or irrelevant parts of a story myself, but I never seem to. Having a good editor is like having a guide in a foreign country. You can either wander around by yourself, or you can ask a professional to point you in the most interesting and useful direction. If you are a writer and don't have a good editor, get one!

I have read versions of this story to countless RCWMS writing groups at Pelican House. It was never a surprise when repeat attenders asked, "Are you still working on that book?" Writing is slow. It takes forever. It just does. All the more need for friends along the way. Thanks to all. A special thanks to one frequent attender, Ethel Radmer, who is often on a path parallel to mine, chasing down organizational issues or knotty pieces of family history. You give me hope.

My Friday writing group has cheered me on in this project for years. Many thanks to Liz Dowling-Sendor, Betty Wolfe, Susan Hazlett, and Marion Thullbery. Keep writing!

I am so blessed to have talented, generous friends without whom my prose would be bumpy and my spelling would be atrocious. A million thanks to those who read versions of the manuscript: Liz Dowling-Sendor, Amy Kellum, Marcy Litle, Kaudie McLean, Ron Moss, Lucy Oliver, Nancy Rosebaugh, and Ethel Simonetti. They did what they could to make the pages clean. Errors that remain are mine.

Many thanks to the grammar queens, Emily Seelbinder and Carolyn Currie Hall. I feel safe in the deep end of the writing pool knowing that when I holler, "Help, help," they will come to the rescue with a comma.

I, have deep admiration and gratitude for Pati Reis, a brilliant graphic designer at Designing Solutions in Durham. She made the book beautiful beyond my wildest dreams.

Frank Stasio let me read a few pages of the book on WUNC's *The State of Things* in April of 2013. Thank you. It was *Flying Over Home*'s first public appearance.

Rachael Wooten, my friend in writing and life, helps to keep me sane. She knows exactly how long and hard one has to work to keep a book project alive and offers constant encouragement by her words and by not giving up on her own project. Watch for her book on Tara, the female Buddha of Tibet.

Dwight Honeycutt, my love, makes life worth living. Thank you.